ECONOMIC PROSPERITY
IN THE BRITISH EMPIRE

ECONOMIC PROSPERITY
IN THE BRITISH EMPIRE

by

STEPHEN LEACOCK

B.A., Ph.D., LL.D., Litt.D., F.R.S.C.

HEAD OF THE DEPARTMENT OF ECONOMICS AND POLITICAL
SCIENCE, McGILL UNIVERSITY MONTREAL

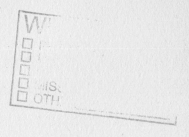

THE MACMILLAN COMPANY
OF CANADA LTD
TORONTO
1930

First Published 1930

Printed in Great Britain by Butler & Tanner Ltd., Frome and London

The title of this book was changed to "ECONOMIC PROSPERITY IN THE BRITISH EMPIRE" too late for an alteration to be made in the running headlines.

CONTENTS

PART I. UNTIL NOW

PART II. FROM NOW ON

PART I
UNTIL NOW

THE ECONOMIC INTEGRATION OF THE BRITISH EMPIRE

CHAPTER I

THE EMPIRE AS A PROPRIETARY ASSET

IT is the purpose of this book to discuss the economic integration of the British Empire. By this is meant the establishment of a system of mutual co-operation for the development of the vast potential wealth of the Empire and for the expansion of its present limited population.

It is no longer possible to aim at complete economic union. For that the day is past. Such a union is probably no longer even desirable. In each of the great Dominions there has been established a system of manufacture and an urban concentration dependent on it, that cannot now be obliterated. But as towards the outside world a uniformity of economic policy may still be achieved ; and the now separated parts of the Empire may co-operate with one another in the use of capital, the movement of population and the development of national resources, with results as yet scarcely

imagined. It is within the reach of statesmanship
to initiate in the British Empire an era of prosperity
and progress such as the world has never yet seen
anywhere at any time.

. . . .

For three generations past, in the name of
"political freedom", British statecraft and colonial
aspirations have set themselves to break up the
Empire into a series of disconnected parts. The
gift of "responsible government" to the colonies,
that began in 1840, carried with it a division of
resources, a separation of public debts, a repudia-
tion of all common obligations, a complete dis-
location of all common action. It was the partition
of an estate. Each of the beneficiaries retired with
his own, to use it or not as each saw fit. Most of
the talents stayed hidden in the ground. The
parent source of capital and migration flowed away
to enrich the United States and Argentina. In the
sixty years from 1840 to 1900, 10,513,000 British
emigrants, or seventy-five per cent of the total,
moved outside of the bounds of the Empire ; only
3,688,000, or twenty-five per cent, migrated to territory under the British Crown.

As a result of all this, what should have been a
united economic commonwealth, comparable to the
United States, but immensely greater, is but a
group of fragments. The vast totality of resources
that is the heritage of all is available to none. A
part of the Empire is crowded to the verge of standing room. Two million idle men look across the
sea at 2,000,000 square miles of empty land. In
some quarters of our disunited commonwealth each

4

single subject of the Crown, as in Western Australia, represents three square miles of land ; elsewhere, as in England itself, his share is less than the five-hundredth part of one square mile.

Nor is there any single authority left that can bring the people to the land or the land to the people. Capital accumulates in Lombard Street while the empty fertile spaces of the outer Empire remain, decade after decade, silent. Western Australia, as large as all of Europe west of Warsaw, lies almost motionless under its own weight. Its little handful of people cannot use more than a fraction of it. Canada, portioned off into half a continent in 1867, staggers forward under its burden ; alternately it falls prone and rises again : each successive " land boom " is followed by a flat collapse. It has never had money enough and men enough for its development. It has thrown about itself an outline apparatus of 40,000 miles of railways, with vast bridges carrying nothing to nowhere and town sites in the grass of the prairies. The frame is too big for the picture. And those who might help fill it in are warned off in the nature of " responsible government ". In the sixty odd years since the Confederation of 1867 Canada has established in its north-west a population of 2,000,000 people. This feat, if we could rightly use our population, capital and resources, could be duplicated in two years.

The same picture of imperfect development and of relative stagnation for lack of capital resources is reflected throughout the Empire. In the temperate uplands of Africa, such an area as Northern Rhodesia, with over a quarter of a million square miles, supports the white population of a country town. The Pacific Islands on the British Columbia coast represent as large a territory, as rich a heritage of resources as the whole Ægean civilization of Greece. The Queen Charlotte Islands alone have an area (3,780 square miles) that is one-third the size of Belgium. The islands possess a temperate climate, magnificent harbours, anthracite and bituminous coal, large forests, prolific fisheries and the population of an English market town—2,000 as against the 7,500,000 people in Belgium. Yet this island group has been in the possession of British people for over a hundred years, scarcely known and utterly unutilized till a few years ago, while four generations of British people at home looked in vain for food and work for all. South Africa, with its agricultural areas scarcely touched, remains quiescent, a heroic land of sorrows, still making its politics out of history and importing food from Australia.

In the West Indies a white population of 50,000 occupies what were once the treasure islands of the world. Here as elsewhere—almost everywhere—in the British Empire, a principal lively hope is placed in the money of the American tourist, for whom all the world is turned into an hotel.

As with the divided resources of the British Empire so with its population. Migration within the Empire is no longer free. It is no longer co-operative. It is no longer under any single control. Quite apart from all questions of the colour line, of the conflict of oriental civilization with western, quite apart from all problems of political freedom

—the white population of the Empire is no longer free to move, except to get out of it. The erroneous doctrine that an empty-handed man is not worth having has carried the day. Economic ignorance has bred legislative restraint : the labour vote helps to shut labour out of its inheritance.

As a result, population in the Empire crowds and congests at the centres. The overcrowding of England begins to be reproduced in the great cities of the Dominions. The gloomy shadow of Malthus falls over the entire scene. The population of Great Britain in each generation of the manufacturing era has been strongly held in check by poverty, by opinion, by lack of economic knowledge and statecraft—in short, by what seemed sheer necessity —at the very period when population was the principal need of the British commonwealth. The unborn British population of the nineteenth century —the children that could have been born from Malthus' time to ours, with the natural increase of humanity, would have reached now a final total of half a billion. Their little ghosts flutter in the ether of our historic background.

And of those born, 10,980,000 went, needlessly and to our detriment, out of the Empire.

.   .   .   .

The lack of economic unity that has thus retarded the development of the British Empire appears all the more striking when we place beside it the contrasted picture of the United States. Here was a country which at the outset of the nineteenth century could not be compared to Great Britain and its dependencies, except in hope. Its population in 1800 was only 5,000,000 as compared with the 16,000,000 of the British Isles. Its territory, prior to the Louisiana purchase of 1803, was only half a million square miles as compared with an approximate 10,000,000 under the British Crown. Its accumulated monetary capital was almost negligible beside that of England. Manufacture was only struggling into existence as between independence and the war of 1812. There were water-power mills in New England spinning yarn still woven on hand-looms. Anthracite coal had been discovered, but no one could melt it, and the settlers used it to make side-walks. For the furnaces and forges that had sprung up in Western Pennsylvania they used bituminous coal from England. Not till the ingenious Joseph Smith applied a forced draught to the "stone coal" did the first outline of the world's greatest industry begin to reveal itself. For fifty years after the Declaration of Independence the manufactures of the United States were as nothing compared to the rising glory of Yorkshire and Lancashire.

Yet the United States, after the adoption of the sagacious constitution of 1789, possessed the supreme advantage of economic unity; and after the Louisiana purchase and the exploits of Clark and Lewis and other pathfinders, its territory reached unbroken from sea to sea. Its population could move, could expand, could multiply without limit. Each application of capital, industrial and monetary, opened the way for more. Immigration after 1840 entered in a flood, each successive wave washing farther across the continent.

Meantime the outlying empire of Great Britain

remained for the most part empty, with no system, and little attempt at any system, for filling it up. In the fortunate United States Nature and circumstances supplied the system. There was no need of a plan. The western frontier moved of itself, like an industrial skirmish of civilization.

. . . .

In the earlier half of the nineteenth century it was perhaps scarcely to be avoided that the migratory population of the British Isles should go to the United States rather than to the unoccupied territory of the greater colonies. Australia was still separated from England by a sailing voyage of six months. The Cape was little more than a port of call mid-way on the Australian voyage. The province of Canada, apart from entry by crossing the United States, was cut off from the world for nearly six months in the year. The empty north-west was unapproachable except by the Hudson Strait, and those who best knew its value kept this knowledge to themselves. To alter this situation would have needed an initial effort beyond the foresight of the times.

But the situation by the latter half of the century had altered of itself. Steam navigation, after the opening of the Suez Canal (1869), cut even the Australian voyage to less than two months, and presently to one. The Atlantic service became a ferry. Gold opened, in turn, Australia, British Columbia and South Africa. The Canadian North-west came within easy reach of lake steamers and Minnesota railways by 1880. At this point the moving flood of capital and migration could have

9

been—should have been—diverted to the empty empire ; the natural expansion of population of the British Isles should have gone unchecked with bread and work for all under the flag, over the seas if not at home. But by this time "responsible government" had done its work. The spiritual insistence on political freedom had dislocated economic unity.

As a result, the increasing wealth and power of the United States foreshadowed with every decade its coming dominance. On the eve of the Civil War the population of the United States (31,000,000) had overtaken and passed that of the British Isles (30,000,000). At the end of the outgoing century it surpassed it as 76,000,000 to 42,000,000.

The economic unity of the United States enabled it to develop its resources in a way unknown in the British Empire. Four transcontinental railways linked up the republic from ocean to ocean, while British North America for hundreds of miles north of Lake Superior had not even a wagon road. Kansas and Nebraska were filling up with farmers, while Alberta, a better country, remained only a game preserve and a buffalo pasture. During all the earlier part, at least, of this development a principal basis for the economic development of the United States was supplied by British capital and by the unending migration from the British Isles. Between the years 1860 and 1900 the United States opened up with railways and land grants the north-west territory represented by the seven northern states that lie between the Mississippi and the Rocky Mountains, an area of 700,000 square miles, and put into it a population of 6,000,000 inhabitants. During that same time the north-west territory of Canada (what is now Manitoba, Saskatchewan and Alberta), a better country with an area almost identical and with higher resources gathered in only 400,000 people. There was no reason for this except our lack of statecraft. With this economic development of the United States has come also a growth of urban population, of manufactures and of wealth that first rivalled, then equalled and then far overpassed, that of Great Britain.

More than that, the American people were earlier to seize the opportunities that arose out of the new environment. They made the motor-car their own. About two-thirds of the 33,000,000 motor-cars in the world belong in the United States, where there is one motor-car for every five people ; in the world at large there is about one to every sixty.

Similarly the moving picture was seized and turned into a world industry. The climate of California—which enjoys advantages very similar to those of Cape Town and Western Australia, with an equal variation of scenery and the similarly fortunate proximity of the sea—supplied the first initial advantage that guided the flood of effort and capital. So may a pebble in a stream divert the course of a river.

As a result, the United States, a country of smaller resources, less territory, less capital and without— let us hope—a superiority of intellect—surpassed in its industrial development its greater rival. This

never should have been. It is for the present
century to reveal whether this condition need
continue.

. . . .

Looking forward, then, towards the prospect
which now confronts the British Empire, one may
best begin with something like an appraisement
of the wealth and the potential wealth, the territory,
resources and the development of the resources
possessed by its people. In doing this the central
point of interest for this present essay lies in the
question of the expansion of the white race, of the
occupation of "white man's territory" and the
outlook for what is called western civilization. It
is no part of the present work to discuss the future
industrial development of the tropical dependencies
of the Empire. Great as is their importance as a
source of wealth, they can never be a part of the
British commonwealth in the higher sense. In such
areas the white race can find no home. They ought
in the one course of time to be handed over to races
fitted for the climate. Still less is it the present
purpose to discuss the future, either economic or
political, of the 325,000,000 mixed Asiatics who live
in British India. It is quite possible that with
advancing industrial technique and with better
organization even this huge population may expand
in number and increase in prosperity. But this is
a problem shared by all crowded industrial countries,
whether Asiatics or European, and has little or
nothing to do with the theme of this book. The
present purpose is to examine the co-ordination of
empty fertile spaces and unused national resources

with the growth and movement of the white population under the British Crown.

. . . .

It is proper to begin with a few generalities, familiar, but so imposing as to stand the wear and tear of repetition. The British Empire represents an area of 13,491,977 square miles, or one-fifth of the land surface of the globe. It carries a population of 450,000,000 people, or one-quarter of the human race. In Australia it owns a continent, in Canada the half of one. Both of these, where habitable at all, are " white man's territories ". In South Africa the Union and its mandate in South-West Africa, with the adjacent country of the two Rhodesias, adds up to 1,250,000 square miles. The uplands of Africa, the cooler regions of the equatorial highlands, Kenya and Uganda, may perhaps also, though perhaps not, turn out to be suitable for permanent white occupation. To all this there is to be added such insular possessions as New Zealand (in area nearly equal to the British Isles), Newfoundland, and, in a sense, the West Indies. But the calculation of the total population under the British Crown is most misleading. Of the grand total of 450,000,000 no less than 325,000,000 belong in British India and Ceylon. Outside of that the population of the rest of the Empire numbers only 125,000,000, and from this we must subtract again the 20,000,000 natives of Nigeria, the 40,000,000 of various African and other dependencies, so that at the end of the count the population of the British Empire, as far as it is white, becomes striking not by its size but by its lack of it. It numbers only

66,500,000—about the same number of people who lived, without overcrowding, in the German Empire of 1914, an area of 208,000 square miles, or rather less than the area of Saskatchewan.

The opportunity for expansion and development thus offered seems at first almost appalling. Here is a population of sixty-six and a half million people with undisputed access to the land and resources of a fifth of the globe. They are recognized by all other Powers, even if with a certain reluctance, as the " owner " of it. They are equipped with the technique of modern production, were themselves the first to invent it, and have control of monetary capital far greater than that of any European nation, as great perhaps indirectly as that of the United States.

The picture becomes still more highly coloured when we turn to enumerate the share of the British peoples in the principal natural commodities that serve as the basis of the world's production of wealth. Of these the first and the most fundamental is arable land. The ploughshare is the earliest emblem of our Western civilization as it arose slowly out of and from the land. On the entire globe there are calculated to be 52,500,000 square miles of land surface, and of this 13,500,000 square miles are in the Empire. Only a fraction of this is now cultivated, in Australia only one per cent, in Canada three per cent. No estimate has ever been made of all the arable land in all the Empire. But from calculations made in regard to Canada, it is certain that in the great Dominions cultivation could easily be multiplied as five to one.

Next to land is coal. Western civilization was not built upon it and knew and cared little about it for the first two thousand years after the rise of Greece and Rome. Its part in the world's history only began about the year 1700. But once utilized as a source of power in the industrial revolution and the eighteenth century, it rapidly assumed a major importance in material civilization.

In the year 1700 England mined and used only about two and a half million tons of coal. At the present time the entire consumption of coal in the world for domestic heat, factory power, railway and marine transport amounts to 1,235,000,000 tons per annum. Of this the United States, now the largest producing country in the world, raises 591,720,000 tons. The British Empire mines each year at present an average of 305,000,000 tons, of which 245,000,000 comes from the British Isles. The first warnings of apprehension in regard to the future supply were heard as far back as the middle of the nineteenth century, when Professor Stanley Jevons in his *Coal Question* (1865) prosecuted an inquiry into the probable exhaustion of our coal mines. For two generations already gloomy prognostications have been uttered to the effect that the British coal supply would presently be exhausted. The same apprehension was voiced again by the Royal Commission on Coal Supplies in 1926. " We look forward," says the report of the Commission, " to a time not far distant when the rate of increase of output will be slower, to be followed be a period of stationary outputs, another and gradual decline ".

But as far as the world at large, or even the

Empire at large is concerned, this apprehension need not be of a lively character. It resembles somewhat the astronomical alarm at the distressing slackening in the motion of the earth, calculated sooner or later to have disastrous consequences for mankind but at present involving only the loss of one second every two or three thousand years. It is probable that long before the exhaustion of world coal occurs, the world will have ceased to use coal.

Here are the facts. The coal beds of the earth are estimated to contain 7,863,556,000,000 metric tons of coal. At the present rate of use it would take humanity many centuries to burn the truly available part of it, and 6,000 years to burn it all if it could be reached. The United States, fortunate above all other nations, possesses a potential supply of 3,536,000,000,000 tons, of which great areas in Pennsylvania, West Virginia and elsewhere are of anthracite, the coal of highest quality and heating power. In other places, as in the Mesabi range in Minnesota, the coal lies so close to the surface that it does not need to be " mined " ; it has only to be shovelled out. In the British Isles, as already said, the total known coal area contains still a supply of 166,000,000,000 tons. But there is no sooner talk of its exhaustion than hope springs up anew with the reports of possible new beds of great potential value under the quiet countryside of South-east England. If the possibility of running out of coal were the chief of England's worries, the country would be happy indeed.

In Canada are vast beds of coal. But it is ill situated. It lies in the extreme east and in the far west and is lacking, pending further discoveries, in Central Canada, the principal area of population and manufacture. The coal beds of Nova Scotia are estimated to contain 2,639,000,000 tons, those of Alberta 12,000,000,000. The dependence of Central Canada upon American coal, of which it imports yearly 16,500,000 tons, is one of the weak spots in the self-protective mechanism of the imperial system. Promising discoveries of coal, in the uninhabited littoral of the James Bay, reported officially by the Government of Ontario in 1929, may prove of vital value as an economic link in a broken chain.

Of the metals one turns first to gold as that of the greatest prestige, the history of which has helped to govern the expansion of Europe. Many modern economists assure us that we could do nicely without it, and that its use as the basis of currency is as antiquated as the stage coach. But public opinion at large still values its possession. Here the British Empire, starting among the last, has become easily the first in production. The discovery of America presently brought to Europe the gold of Mexico and Peru. There was but little of it, as we count our gold now. But in the world of Christopher Columbus's day, with perhaps no more than the coin equivalent of $160,000,000 of gold and silver in all, and with older sources of supply washed out, it appeared as fabulous wealth. Spain, as between 1500 and 1600, drew about $5,000,000 of gold per annum from the mines of Central and South America. By the middle of the nineteenth century gold production reached $118,000,000 a year, and the accumulated supply, perhaps $200,000,000. Then came the discovery of the California gold which ran soon to an annual output of $56,000,000 and which at the present day still amounts to $12,000,000. The Australian gold fields of Victoria (1851) soon rivalled those of California, and reached in 1853 a maximum output of $60,000,000. Australia, including the gold diggings of Victoria, Tasmania, and Western Australia, produced (1909) only a little more than this total, and has since sunk to an output of $10,000,000, almost nine-tenths of it from Western Australia.

But South Africa presently eclipsed all other gold fields and still leads the world. The Witwatersrand, a great ridge of buried gold ore on a plateau in the Central Transvaal, is estimated to have produced, up till 1926, a total gold value of about $4,500,000,000, and at present produces annually about $200,000,000, or more than half of all the gold mined in the world. In Canada the gold produced until recent years was negligible in the world's supply. British Columbia, where gold was discovered in 1858, represented at its highest point (1913) an output of $6,149,027. The discoveries in the Yukon Territory turned the eyes of the world to the Gold Rush to the Klondyke in 1898, and built up Dawson " City " to a temporary population of 20,000 inhabitants. The gold boom passed as it came, pending further good fortune in the Arctic wilderness still only partly explored. But the gold of Northern Ontario, lying in the Lake Temiskaming district, has become a rising factor in the world's supply. Beginning with $42,000 in 1911, it has reached an annual output of over $32,000,000.

Taken all in all, the civilized world is estimated to possess in coin and gold a quantity that is equivalent to about 17,000,000,000 gold dollars. The annual production, averaged for the ten years since the war, amounts to $412,000,000. The output of the year 1927 was $410,000,000. For the same ten years the British Empire averages seventy per cent of the total. For the year 1927 the total Empire output was $290,000,000 ; and that of the rest of the world, $120,000,000 ; South Africa, $209,000,000 ; Canada, $38,000,000 ; Australia, $13,000,000. The production of the United States was $46,000,000. Thus over seventy per cent of the world's gold is provided by the British Empire, a percentage which in all likelihood is destined to a further and continuous increase.

Iron comes next. Here the world at large is blest with one of the few supplies which we still dare call "inexhaustible". Vast deposits of iron ore exist all over the globe, many of them, such as those of inland Brazil, as yet untouched, and beyond the present reach of man. From those in use the world extracts each year about 146,000,000 tons. From the Mesabi Range in Minnesota, where the ore lies close to the surface, about 35,000,000 tons are shovelled up every year. Altogether 780,000,000 tons have been taken out. The geological department of the state of Minnesota estimates that there are still 1,250,000,000 tons left. From the great iron deposits of the Franco-German borderland a similar quantity, at present about 37,000,000 tons of ore, is raised annually. In the iron deposits that underlie the North of England, north of a line drawn from Yorkshire to Dorset, there are said to be 3,400,000,000 tons of workable ore. But when all these resources are gone the world, at large, has no occasion to worry. Geologists tell us that the workable ore beds of the globe comprise 30,000,000,000 tons. With a present annual utilization of 146,000,000 tons, we can see our way ahead for about two hundred years. After that—but that is far enough.

For the first hundred years of the modern industrial era Great Britain led the world in the production of iron. Indeed the rise of the iron and steel industry was one of the largest features of the industrial revolution. In Queen Anne's reign England only produced each year a few thousand tons of iron. About 18,000 tons of pig iron were produced by 1740. In 1820 the entire world production ran to a million tons ; in 1850 about four and three quarter million tons. Of these Great Britain produced two and a quarter million and the United States only 630,000 tons. But between the years 1880 and 1890 the United States industry, stimulated by the protective tariff and organized on a basis of mechanical transport and manufacture never seen before, overtook the British with giant strides, passed it and left it presently in relative insignificance. In 1890 the United States produced 9,000,000 tons of pig iron and Great Britain less than 8,000,000. In 1928 the figures stood at 37,800,000 against 6,500,000.

It is not necessary to deal with the other minerals in the same detail. But a glance at the table of the world's mineral output which is here appended will illustrate the general position. In certain cases the

British Empire enjoys an overwhelming superiority in the possession of mineral resources. Extreme cases are those of cobalt, asbestos and nickel. Cobalt is a metal, unknown till yesterday to the industry and commerce of the world, but now of great utility for advanced forms of steel manufacture and for the making of pigments for the linoleum manufactures. The entire world's supply is in the Empire, the greater part of it coming from the deposits of Northern Ontario.

In asbestos, Quebec and South Africa supply ninety-five per cent of the world's consumption; in nickel, the northern districts of Ontario and Saskatchewan enjoy an overwhelming advantage: in the last ten years Canada has produced from eighty-seven to ninety per cent of the world's output. With certain other minerals and metals, though to a lesser degree, the advantage is all the other way. Of copper the British Empire only produces four and one half per cent of the annual supply, though there is every prospect of a great wealth of copper ore being discovered between the Hudson Bay and the Copper Mine River in Arctic Canada. Almost the whole of the world's quicksilver (99·8) per cent comes from Spain; sulphur and phosphates from the United States and the world's nitrate from Chile.

But the case of extreme importance is that of petroleum, the basis of the now universal gasolene, without which, under present conditions, the industrial life of any nation comes to a full stop. It seems strange now to look back to the despised " rock oil ", which was about a hundred years ago oozing out on the surface of the marshlands of the Pennsylvania valleys and floating on the ponds. The early settlers could find no use for it except as a liniment for sores and burns. Then a certain Mr. Ker purified it enough to burn it in a " coal oil " lamp as " kerosene ". Chemists distilled it. Naphtha, benzine and paraffin flared upon the market. Industrial capital sank wells and pumped it out. The 2,000 barrels of 1857 had become 150,000,000 barrels at the end of the century. Then came the invention of the explosive engine, making possible the aeroplane and the motor-car. Rock oil became the most conspicuously important product in the world. All the world was ransacked to find it, and up to now it is the hard fate of the British Empire to be away behind in the supply. The whole world produced in 1927 a total of 1,254,145,000 barrels, of which 905,000,000, or seventy-two per cent, came from the United States. Next stood Russia with 5·77 per cent, Venezuela with 5·12 per cent. British India is set down at 8,200,000 barrels, or less than half of one per cent of the world's supply, and beyond that the Empire is clean out of it. Canada, with half a million barrels, makes only an insignificant contribution.

The case, however, is not as bad as it seems. Our present dependence on the outside world may easily lessen and disappear. There are various fields within the confines of the British Empire which may prove of great wealth in oil. It would be strange if it were not so. The province of Alberta lies over a vast bed of coal : natural gas exists in great quantities. All geological indications point to the

presence of oil-bearing strata as yet unrevealed.
Even now oil is produced in promising quantities
in the foothills of the Rocky Mountains, and it is
likely that far to the north of the Alberta in the
valley of the Mackenzie River the small discoveries
of oil already made will prove only a beginning.
Australia still seeks petroleum in vain. But there
is oil in British Borneo, most probably in Papua,
certainly in New Zealand (but with the quantity in
doubt), and undoubtedly, and in large quantities,
in the West Indian island of Trinidad. Another
generation, another decade, may alter the entire
outlook.

Another commodity, like petroleum of little
significance to the world till yesterday, is rubber.
Though known and used for a century, it had little
place in the greater manufactures. Even in 1910
the world's annual consumption was only about
3,000 tons. Goodyear's discovery of " hot vulcaniza-
tion " goes back as far as 1839, but it is only of late
years that processes have been devised for combining
rubber with other materials (fabrics, metals, glass,
wood, etc.) so as to secure both elasticity and
strength. The development of the motor-car both
stimulated and utilized these processes. The
production of rubber in 1927 reached over 622,000
British tons, an increase which is not an end but
apparently only a beginning. Almost the whole
of the rubber supply at present originates from
rubber trees ; the manufacture of synthetic rubber,
as in Germany, from lime and coke by a complicated
chemical process is yet of small commercial importance. The principal natural forests are in the

valley of the Amazon, with lesser sources of supply in Central America and the East Indies, Siam, French Indo-China and Siberia. But the world's rubber supply no longer comes to any great extent from the natural forests. About ninety-five per cent of it is drawn from " plantations " of rubber trees, the greater part of them grown in Malaya and other British tropical dependencies. The Empire produces about seventy-five per cent of the world's rubber. But when it comes to the manufacture of rubber, into motor tyres and other goods, the situation is reversed. The Empire is relatively out of it. The United States uses about seventy per cent of the world's rubber, which thus becomes the basis of one of its greatest industries, with an output valued at over one and a quarter billion dollars.

.   .   .   .

A most imposing asset of the British Empire which seems to carry in the very sound of it the voice of the future is the asset of the waterfall, the rapid and the river—the tremendous potentiality of water-power. Coal and petroleum are sources of power, but the present industrial world looks more and more to the electrical energy to be developed from falling water.

Statistics of potential power are often of little meaning to the ordinary reader from the want of an elementary understanding of the units concerned. It is customary to estimate the actual and potential use of falling water in terms of " horse-power ". This method of calculation originated with Mr. James Watt of the eighteenth century, inventor and patentee of the first practicable steam engine. By a " horse-power " he meant the amount of work performed by a first-class cart-horse, which he set as equivalent to raising 33,000 pounds through one foot in one minute. A cart-horse which could really do this and keep on doing it would be a rare and valuable beast indeed. But that is of no consequence. The unit, once established, is as good as any other. In the measurement of electric current and power, as applied and sold commercially, the mechanical horse-power unit is changed for the technical electric unit the watt, of which 746 equal one horse-power. In all general estimates of water-power, actual and potential, the horse-power unit is the common form of calculation. It is estimated that at the present time the world demands for power represents about 120,000,000 horse-power—the amount of energy needed for all the industries, all the transport, both on land and sea ; in short, all the work of the world to which mechanical power is applied. All the factories of all the world are computed to use 75,000,000 horse-power.

The development of the world's water-power is one of the great outstanding features of human achievement in the last twenty years. Of the 30,000,000 horse-power of electrical energy now used in the world about 20,000,000 has been developed since 1900. Modern hydraulic turbines can use any fall of from 10 to 5,000 feet and the electric power, up to pressures of 220,000 volts, can be effectively transmitted for distances up to 300 miles.

No estimate of value can be made of the physically potential energy of the world's supply of water falling or ready to fall. But the estimates made are for " available " water-power, meaning power in known and accessible sites that have been made the subject of more or less definite calculation, afford at least a basis of comparison. On this basis it appears that the " available " water-power of the world amounts to 240,000,000 horse-power, of which 30,000,000 is now developed. The power available in the British Empire is 68,000,000, of which nearly one half is in Canada, which has a water area of rivers and lakes equal to 142,674 square miles. It is probable that the figures of " available " power greatly understate the case for Canada. Power re-sources in the United States and in Europe are on the whole better known and more definitely calculated. Immense reserves of power still run unheeded and scarcely known in the northern wilder-nesses of the Dominion. The latest official Canadian statistics show a development of 5,349,232 horse-power, of which 4,290,830 is in Quebec and in Ontario. Water-power in Great Britain is negligible as a prime national asset, but New Zealand, with 3,800,000 horse-power, and South Africa stand high. In Australia a better conservation of the rainfall would create large sources of power, and at the same time serve to irrigate many million acres of land. The Murrum-bridgee irrigation project will create a lake of over 12,000 acres ; the damning of the Goulheim River will irrigate 868,000 acres in the State of Victoria, with a corresponding electrical development.

. . . .

Such, then, is the general aspect of this globe, on which, according to the latest estimates, 2,000,000,000 human beings seek economic livelihood. The picture is still one of collective plenty. Humanity, in spite of the gloomy forebodings of the pessimist, is still a long way from starvation. If we are crowded and unhappy, the fault is ours. Nature is still bountiful enough. The statement has been recently widely circulated in the Press that bio-chemists claim that the potential food supply of the globe would feed 500,000,000,000 people. If so, it seems we are only beginning. In any case when we pass from the general heritage of all the inhabitants of the world to the special heritage of the sixty-six and a half million lucky people who " own " the white man's Empire, the prospect changes from that of plenty to that of profusion. For each of us it seems there is nearly a tenth of a square mile of land (64 acres)—without making any claim on the ice-fields or the deserts or the territory of British India or the tropical dependencies of the Africans. Each of us has coal for 2,000 years and all the iron we need for 200. And for each one of the 66,000,000 of us the equivalent of one horse-power permanently at our service —the labour of ten men.

.   .   .   .

Contrast this generous picture of our unused wealth with the notion of overcrowding and the menace of population which haunts the mind of the civilized world, and impresses itself on our public policy and our domestic life.

.   .   .   .

In 1798 a clergyman of the Church of England, the Reverend Thomas Robert Malthus, wrote an *Essay on Population* which led to the disastrous idea that the world was getting crowded. It appeared that the cause of industrial poverty lay in our increasing numbers. The idea, as translated into popular thought, was gloomy in the extreme. It bid defiance to all hope of general profusion and universal comfort. It set stern limits to our material happiness, and gave us poverty and want as the inevitable accompaniment of Western civilization. At the moment when the technique of machine production had opened the gates of a Garden of Eden, Malthus closed them. The shadow of his book still lies dark on the surface of the world. It is time that humanity, and above all that the British peoples, should come out into the sunlight. Our world, at least, is for the most part still empty and untenanted, waving with trees and murmuring with water, awaiting the uncounted millions of unborn children who are to occupy it.

CHAPTER II

THE POSSIBLE EXPANSION OF THE WHITE RACE WITHIN THE BRITISH EMPIRE

SUCH, then, as described above, is the affluent heritage of the British Empire. To what extent is there room for the white population to expand and multiply in the vast territories which they are fortunate enough to own? Canada has now 10,000,000 inhabitants. How many more can be taken in? Australia has six and a half million. How much room is left? How nearly full is New Zealand with 1,454,000 inhabitants?

The true answer to these questions is so different from the current thought of humanity as to be, quite literally, staggering. I propose to show that Canada, even with our present limited industrial technique, can quite easily maintain 200,000,000 inhabitants; that the overseas dominions, in all, can undoubtedly support half a billion inhabitants; and that such a population can be placed there as fast as natural increase and migration can bring them. The capital apparatus needed for the operation is already in existence, is waiting.

But it is not possible to bring forward such a statement without first attempting to clear away something of the murky atmosphere of error and misconception in which the brilliant successes and the hidden failures of nineteenth-century industrialism have landed us.

. . . .

Mankind, so the psychologists assure us, live more and more under the dominance of mass ideas. We all think the same thing at the same time. We carry with us unconsciously the mind of our generation. Just as cloud and sunshine move across a landscape, so do our mass ideas come and go. In the sixteenth century all the world shuddered at a witch, believed in a miracle and bought and sold a slave. Now a witch is only a decrepit old woman, muttering imbecile fancies, and a man who works a miracle is called a crook and goes to jail. The world's thought has passed on, into other sunlight and newer shadows.

And among the mass ideas of our time is the obsession of a crowded world. Stamped into the basis of our common thought is the conviction that humanity has got to limit its numbers ; that to let loose the full natural increase of mankind would mean pauperism and ruin ; that the world is already so nearly filled up that only collective prudence can save it. We seem to see the symbol of all this in the limited family, the childless apartment and the pecuniary penalties of parenthood. But what we see is an entirely false and misleading phenomenon. It is confusion between the economics of the household and the economics of the world. A family of six or eight children reared on a small income represents a narrow margin of survival. A rash marriage at the dawn of adult life and a cradleful of rasher

children would spell inevitable disaster, a fall into
the abyss of the submerged class. We are so used
to this as a collective idea that we take it for granted.
We do not realize that there must be something
wrong with it ; that it is contrary to every sane
idea of a normal human being. In time, perhaps,
we may get a " survival instinct " to help it : a baby
may appear as hideous as a toad to the " normal "
young man and woman of the year 3000. But that
time is not yet. Meantime, we never stop to ask
whether this individual inhibition has anything to
do with the question of the world's resources and
its capacity to maintain the race. If we did, we
would see that resources do not come into it. It
is a matter of deficient social organization. Our
wants could easily be satisfied for centuries yet, if
we knew how to see about it.

It was, as already said, the famous *Essay* of
Malthus (1798) which first threw into a high light
the idea of over-population. Malthus lived in the
sudden and perplexing prospect of new wealth
contrasted with new poverty, of factories and
paupers, dividends and poor rates. And he mis-
interpreted it all. His silly dictum that numbers
increase faster than subsistence, that humanity
increases faster than food, is exactly the reverse
of truth. Our food increases faster than we do.
A grain of wheat with its full potential chance multiplies a hundred to one every four months. One
grain in a year turns into a million. One egg laying
oyster once started and encouraged to the full, would
develop within ten years, a progeny that would
require the symbol for infinity to indicate it. Man

cannot begin to keep up with his food in this machine age. He has to stop planting it and turn to a wilderness of other activities. In the complex organization of these, appears unemployment, want and lack of food. But this through no lack of basic resources to produce it. What Malthus thought a phenomenon of nature is only a phenomenon of social organization. True it is, that if the race increased long enough and fast enough, the time would come when there would be no room for it on the globe. But that period is far away and the increase of mankind so limited in various ways not connected with its food that there is no need for so long a look.

This notion of the limitation of numbers applies least of all to the people of the British Empire, whose territory and resources, as far as the white race is concerned, is as yet but little used. We may, therefore, address ourselves with confidence to the idea of calculating just how large a population the Empire can support. For this we need make no discounts on the future advances of science, no anticipation of what will be the effect of new sources of power, of synthetic food and the stabilization of industrial society. We can take things as they are and the prospect is good enough.

Here first is the Dominion of Canada, with 10,000,000 people occupying three and half million square miles. What is the place good for? How much of it is habitable, what can we make it look like in a hundred years?

We may talk first in terms of the climate of Canada and the inhabitability of the country as apart from its resources. The myth of the Canadian climate dies hard. The sneer of a disappointed Frenchman over the " lost acres of snow " got into our history and stayed there. Writing as late as 1848 the English historian Alison speaks of the hopeless desolation of British North America. " Probably seven-eighths of this immense surface," he says, " are doomed to eternal sterility from the excessive severity of the climate, which yields only a scanty herbage to the reindeer, the elk and the musk ox." Even now few people in England realize that in point of latitude the most populous part of Canada is not a northern country at all. If England were slid along the parallels of latitude it would pass—even the most southern point of it—500 miles north of Toronto. London would pass north of Winnipeg, and the island of Great Britain would nicely lie north and south in the province of Saskatchewan. Nearly all of Norway—the part from Oslo, the capital, upwards, lies north of all the Canadian Western provinces—begins, that is, where Alberta ends.

People who have only lived in the gloom of an English winter can form no idea of the charm of the longer days, and the bright winter sunshine in Ontario. Winnipeg, let us say, at times, is frightfully cold. But London is at times frightfully foggy and Rome frightfully hot. Yet in all of these the white race lives, flourishes and multiplies.

False ideas in regard to the coldness of a climate originate from the forbidding aspect of an empty country as yet devoid of shelter, light and the company of mankind. The intense cold seems to the intrepid explorer to strike to his very bones. The still ice of the frozen lakes groans and reverberates beneath the dead light of the aurora borealis. The fierce blizzard cuts against the skin and blinds the vision. It is a picture of terror ; to linger, to stumble, to fall asleep spells death.

Such must have seemed three hundred years ago on a bitter winter night the site of the city of Montreal. But compare it now. As I write this chapter the thermometer stands at about twenty degrees below zero—twenty or twenty-five, it doesn't matter —in short, what is called in England fifty degrees of frost. Yet I look out over a vast city, bright with a myriad lights and animated with the life of a million inhabitants. Other such cities will rise— are rising now—all the way from here to where the Mackenzie River washes into the Arctic Sea.

To fortify a pictured vision with the solid frame of statistics, let it be said that, apart from the Arctic Archipelago, almost the whole of Canada lies within the temperate zone. A glance at the map herewith shows the isothermal line for mean July temperate of sixty degrees (Fahrenheit) drawn across the map of Canada. If this line were drawn across the British Isles, it would traverse the centre of Ireland and pass across England in the latitude of Liverpool. In Canada, in a rough-and-ready way it corresponds, or at least approximates, to the settled and habitable area of the provinces, as opposed to the northern or doubtful territory where population certainly will always be restricted below the European density.

To come to closer details. Let it be noticed first

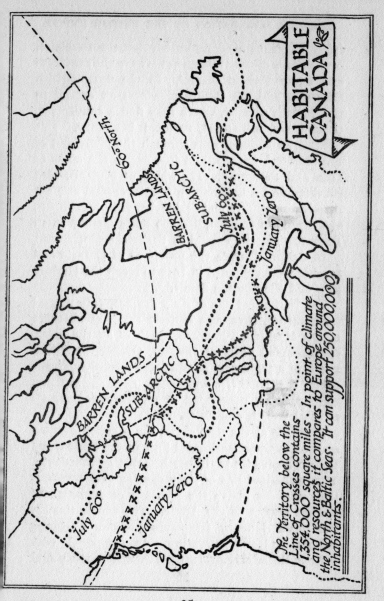

HABITABLE CANADA

60° North

BARREN LANDS

SUB-ARCTIC

July 60°

January Zero

BARREN LANDS

SUB-ARCTIC

July 60°

January Zero

The Territory below the Line of Crosses contains 1,354,000 square miles · In point of climate and resources it compares to Europe around the North & Baltic Seas. It can support 250,000,000 inhabitants.

for convenience of identification that the Dominion of Canada is divided in area as between the provinces and under Federal control. In the west, British Columbia and the Prairie provinces all extend to the sixtieth parallel, where they find a convenient, though not a natural, national boundary. This parallel, in Europe, runs through the lower end of the Shetland Islands, and just passes the cities of Oslo and Petrograd. The whole of Finland, with its three and a half million people, capital and all, is north of Alberta and Saskatchewan. Stockholm, the capital of Sweden, lies 500 miles farther north than Regina, the capital of Saskatchewan.

In Central Canada the provinces of Ontario and Quebec were extended in 1912 to reach the Hudson Bay and the Hudson Strait.

The isothermal line of sixty degrees, July normal temperature, thus runs entirely north of all three of the Maritime Provinces, north of all the older, the occupied parts of Ontario, Quebec, and even north of a large part of what was recently thought of as the northern wilderness, now eagerly and rapidly being penetrated in all directions for its mineral wealth and its forests.

A glance at the map shows the peculiar bending of the Canadian isothermal lines in the middle and their sweeping lift to the north as they go westwards. The isothermal line of sixty degrees July temperature runs far above the province of Alberta and reaches almost to the Arctic. The winter line for the mean January temperature shows a similar though a lesser curvature. As compared with Europe the winter cold strikes farther to the south.

The line of zero (thirty-two degrees of frost) may be taken as the basis of comparison and measurement. There is nothing unhabitable about this; it is the winter temperature of the city of Duluth and Winnipeg and Edmonton. But in Europe the isothermal line of January zero runs away to the north of the British Isles and traverses no other country than Northern Russia. The territory of Canada that lies to the south of the summer isothermal line of sixty degrees would contain approximately one half of its area, or not very far from 2,000,000 square miles. This means that there is at least that much of Canada absolutely and entirely suited for the white race in point of having sufficient warmth in summer.

The winter isothermal lines are not so favourable. The top half of Manitoba, Alberta and Saskatchewan has to be content with a January temperature of ten below zero. But in so large a country there must be some cold corners. And ten below zero menaces neither human life nor human happiness.

So much for the data in point of climate. Now turn to the question of natural productions—the soil, the forests, the grain. We start from the right and move left across the map. Here is first the Labrador Peninsula, about half of which, since the Privy Council decision of 1927, lies outside of Canada. Most of Labrador is a treeless district, a vast total area of over half a million square miles of denuded rocks with forest growth still struggling northward in the valleys, but nowhere reaching the Hudson Strait. Such value as this territory will have, will depend on its mineral wealth, and the possible transmission of water-power. As a home, it seems about as cheerful as Spitzbergen.

A similar area is seen in the " Barren Grounds ", the north-eastern corner of the North-west Territory. A slanting line drawn from Fort Churchill to the valley of the Coppermine River marks it off. It is a country of, perhaps, a quarter of a million square miles of unending emptiness, with great rivers, rushing in summer under the Arctic sunlight and never shaded by a tree. In winter it is a desolation of snow, its lakes and lesser rivers frozen, silent, and embedded. In summer its thin soil is a great verdant carpet of grass, broken with barren protruding rock and gay with a myriad of flowers. The mosquito, breeding in infinite millions, disputes every foot of its possession. Yet even this " barren land " is now known to contain great mineral wealth, and may yet represent in the future a vast pasture for domesticated musk-oxen and deer.

North of the Hudson Bay and Hudson Strait lies the great archipelago of the polar seas, including such areas as Baffin Land, Victoria Land and Ellesmore Island, in all some half a million square miles. The territory claimed by Canada runs like a gore of orange peel to the pole itself. If a ring were drawn around the protruding axis of the earth, we in Canada " own " seventy-five degrees, or more than one-fifth of it. Nor is there at present any lively contention of our claim. From Baffin Land Martin Frobisher brought home in 1578 what he thought was a shipload of gold. Here eager ambition sought a north-west passage to Cathay, a transit actually achieved by Raold Amundsen in

1903–7, long after all possibility of a commercial value of such a route had passed away. Here, perhaps, in the future may be established the airports and emergency stations of a trans-polar route from America to Europe. Here, too, may some day be found mineral wealth. But for proximate purposes the whole of this vast area can be left out of count.

Below all the northern territory thus indicated, there lies in a great curve like a sickle around the Hudson Bay the forest area and the farming area, actual and future, of the central Dominion. We can trace on the map the traversing lines that indicate the northern limits of growth. In the Niagara and Lake Erie districts peaches grow in orchards without great intensive care and with no special winter protection, a thing unknown in the British Isles, save in the half-tropical climate of the Scilly Isles. Anywhere in Southern Ontario melons and tomatoes ripen in open fields. The fruit-growing area of Canada is but a small part of its total territory, and yet if we put together the fruit lands of the Annapolis Valley in Nova Scotia, the Niagara Peninsula and Southern Ontario, and the Okanagan Valley and similar districts in British Columbia it represents in all perhaps 10,000 square miles, an area larger than Wales.

But most important of all the agricultural assets of Canada is the wheat land, actually in use and still waiting its occupants. The wheat plant improves as it goes north, maturing and hardening with the longer sunshine. Wherever the wheat plant can grow, the human race can find its most congenial home, warm enough for comfort and cold enough for vigour, with a soil fertile enough for every stable product of the temperate zone. The " wheat line " lies low in the centre of Canada ; reaching to Lake St. John in the province of Quebec and the North Bay in Ontario, touches the " clay belt " and vanishes into Lake Superior. It reappears at about fifty degrees north latitude in Eastern Manitoba, and lifts magnificently as it runs west, passing north of Alberta. Included in the wheat belt in the Peace River country, a vast potential farm country of 47,000,000 acres, of which as yet only 10,000,000 acres have been surveyed and only 1,331,000 granted to settlers. The wheat crop of Canada has already reached a record of 500,000,000 bushels in a season. Physically it could be multiplied about five to one by cultivating new land. The Canadian Government estimates that of the 1,400,000,000 acres in the land surface of the nine provinces, about 358,000,000 are fit to be farm lands. Of this only 140,000,000 is now in farm use, and of this again only one half is what is officially designated "improved", that is, cultivated land. In addition to this more intensive cultivation could raise the present output per acre (spring wheat in the north-west averages over a period of years about sixteen to twenty bushels) to anything up to double. Indeed, the raising of western wheat in Canada has at present outstripped and overbalanced the national economy. The line of the growth of oats and hay and peas, a further outpost of human sustenance, reaches even farther north than wheat and extends to the James and Hudson Bays and the Barren Lands.

Running across the map of Canada from coast to

coast, rising and falling with the isothermal line of January cold, appears the northern limit of the trees. Each struggles upwards and onwards, to perish almost to the last one before they reach the shores of the Arctic ocean. The fruit-trees vanish first. The hardwood forest—the maples and the beeches and the elms—go next, the forty-ninth parallel, except for British Columbia, being about their upper limit. The greatest woodland glory of Central Canada is gone. The huge pine-trees that rose among the settlements of the Loyalists have no counterpart to-day, except in the timbered areas of British Columbia. But the lesser pine-trees and the largest and best spruce grow in Central Canada half-way to the James Bay and in the west half-way up Manitoba and to the northern boundary of Alberta. Beyond that the coniferous forests of lesser spruce and tamarack, mixed with birch and willow and alder, reach to sea water around the James Bay and only die out at the edge of the Barren Lands. Down the Mackenzie valley a few trees reach almost, and the scrub willow quite, to the polar sea. Take it all in all, the timber lands of the Dominions, as officially reported, cover 1,151,454 square miles and contain 224,000,000,000 feet of timber.

Put beside all this the amount of the agricultural land—occupied and awaiting occupation, which is estimated by the Government of Canada at 358,000,000 acres, 550,000 square miles, or five times the present cultivated area of farm lands. Add to it the one and a quarter million metric tons of coal computed to lie under the surface of the Dominion and the vast treasures of gold and silver, nickel and copper now being opened up, and the picture is one of colossal resources, as yet hardly broken in upon.

Taking as the data the elements thus presented, we are in a position to make a rough estimate of the population that can be put into Canada. We are concerned only with the area that compares in general physical climate and resources to Western and Northern Europe. In this area we may include, starting from the west, the whole of British Columbia without any deduction. The mountain ranges of the Rockies and the Selkirks are just as much and just as little a bar to human habitation as the Alps, the Carpathians and the mountains of Norway and Sweden. British Columbia contains 353,000 square miles.

We include the whole of Alberta and of Saskatchewan. The drier area of the southern part of Alberta and its sister province—once flatteringly called the " Great Desert of the Saskatchewan "— will yield to irrigation and improved methods by our farming. Civilization and closer settlement will obviously go beyond the northern boundaries of Alberta and follow the forests and the coal beds down the Great Slave basin and the valley of the Mackenzie. It is already doing so. But we may use this extra piece of habitable territory to offset the doubtful parts of Saskatchewan, and hence in our estimate include the whole of the land area of both provinces, an extent of 491,000 square miles.

But for its mineral wealth, Northern and Northeastern Manitoba might well stay empty for ever. But the Hudson Bay Railway and Ocean route is now creating a sea port at Fort Churchill. The

Flin Flon mine and its adjacent district, known all the way to Wall Street, lies in latitude fifty-five degrees north. But mineral wealth is, after all, conjectural, and the permanently frozen soil and intense cold of the northern and eastern part of Manitoba must leave perhaps one quarter of the area of the province outside of our present count and give an available land area of 180,000 square miles.

On the extreme east of Canada the entire area of the three maritime provinces, in all 50,000 square miles, may be properly included. But the estimate of the potential settlement of Ontario and Quebec offers great difficulties. Ontario has an area of 365,000 square miles of land, and presents almost incredible variations of climate and fertility. Its most southerly point is almost in the latitude of Barcelona in Spain. At the north, where it extends along the Hudson Bay, it reaches the latitude of Northern Denmark. In the Niagara district and along Lake Erie peaches ripen in the open air. The western peninsula and the Lake Ontario district is a land of wheat and of mixed farming, capable of intensive cultivation. In the centre the land over the divide where the rivers run to the James Bay is a mournful lowland of marsh and muskeg with stunted forest, falling to a shallow and inhospitable sea. Between Lake Superior and the Hudson Bay is a tangled wilderness of rock, lake, river and secondary forest—of vast interest for its minerals, but rugged and cold in the extreme. White River station, just north of Lake Superior, with a record low temperature of sixty degrees below zero, could enter into competition with any place as the coldest inhabited spot in all the world.

If one had to work out an estimate to show what part of the province can be classed as similar to Western Europe as an economic and climatic basis of settlement, it might be done in a rough-and-ready way by including all of the territory south of the Transcontinental Railway and disregarding everything (even the miners and the prospectors and the aeroplanes) that lies and flies to the north of it. But it would be difficult to estimate the area of this, and therefore I propose the simpler method of including, for the present purpose, one-half of Ontario, and then making a comparison by throwing into the scale in Western Europe land equally rugged and equally cold.

For Quebec a similar difficulty arises. Its area is vast. Even after the subtraction made of the Privy Council decision of 1927, which gave Eastern Labrador to Newfoundland, there is an area of 583,000 square miles of land. The province has a sea coast of some 900 miles, along the James and Hudson Bays and the Hudson Strait. A vast part of the northern territory is unknown, is problematical, or worse. Mineral wealth is being discovered, and claims established, anywhere and everywhere in the wilderness. But beyond this, great areas seem destined to emptiness—at least until the Malthusian " standing-room only " is reached in some dim future. Agriculture flourishes in the south in the " eastern townships " of the American border, and dies out rapidly on the north side of the St. Lawrence. But the Lake St. John district and Peribonka valley

(immortalized by Maria Chapdelaine) is one of farms
and fields (not wheat), and everywhere the forests
of pulp wood attract settlement of the great companies. Such towns as that of Kenogami and
Chicoutimi, built more or less ready-made by pulp
and paper companies, seem to have sprung up over-
night. But a possible boundary for the present
purpose can be found in following the height of land
between the James and Hudson Bays and the St.
Lawrence, as far as Lake St. John, and thence due
east till the lines reach the St. Lawrence River.
This is a conventional line ; but an authoritative
estimate is not available. South of this line the
whole country is habitable and, with variations,
fertile. Even north of it, there is much.

Such a division leaves an area for Quebec of only
about 100,000 square miles, a most conservative
estimate, since it takes in only one-sixth of the province, and this, put along with that of the other
provinces, gives a total area in Canada available for
white settlement of 1,354,000 square miles. At present it is occupied by 10,000,000 people, or 25 to
the square mile. How many people per square
mile can such territory potentially support ?

. . . .

The calculation of potential population per square
mile is one not easy to undertake with assurance.
But a few general lines of approach may be indicated.
If we take as the maximum some of the denser areas
of the inhabited world, such as the county of Middle-
sex or the island of Manhattan, we find that population may run to hundreds of thousands to the square
mile. Even outside of metropolitan areas we find

45

such examples as the kingdom of Belgium with 675, the island of Java with 720, and Barbados with nearly 1,000 persons to the square mile. The metropolitan areas are of course drawing their basic support, in terms of resources, from outside territory. We leave them out of count. Even in the case of a whole country we cannot always look upon the whole population as drawing its whole support from the resources of its territories. Take the case of Switzerland. A large part of the activity of the Swiss consists in the entertainment of visitors. They lodge them, feed them, show them Mont Blanç and take them ski riding. Switzerland has an annual adverse trade balance of about a hundred million dollars, representing the money annually spent in Switzerland by the tourists. A part of this is accounted for by the purchase of Swiss food raised in Switzerland. But the rest of it, indeed the greater part of it, represents a payment in money (presently turned into imported goods) for services that do not correspond in the economic resources of the country. It is only in the artistic sense and not in the economic that the poet or the painter consumes the resources of Switzerland.

Or take the case of the United Kingdom. It contains at present about forty-five and a half million people. But a great many of them do not live on the natural resources of the country. The United Kingdom had (before the War) $20,000,000,000 of outside investments, has even now certainly three-quarters as much. Many people live on the interest of this —the interest taking the visible form of imported commodities. The United Kingdom has 20,000,000 tons of shipping, and does a carrying trade far beyond the proportion of its production and consumption ; hence many people (sailors and their families, owners, shareholders, official staffs) live on this. More than that, England imports enormous quantities of raw material—cotton, etc.—and works it into finished goods. Millions live on that. It would not do to say that because the United Kingdom contains 481 people per square mile, therefore Western Ontario, which is, on the whole, as fertile, could do the same. It couldn't ; unless history and circumstances put it in the peculiar industrial position of England. If all the people were swept away, England and its distinctive situation ended, it would not be possible to put another lot back, equally numerous, to live on the resources of the island.

All of this needs to be said, elementary though it sounds, to avoid statistical error in multiplying out potential population in the British Dominions.

Consider again the case of Belgium. Here live 7,932,000 people, or 675 to the square mile. It is a country of intense and intensive cultivation of the soil, of land drained and improved and utilized to the last degree. Perhaps the greater part of the population live directly or indirectly on the land and its produce. This does not mean that they are all farmers : the shopkeepers of a village where the farmers (and no others) deal, a gendarme who keeps the farmers (and no one else) in order, a preacher who exhorts the farmers (and no one else) is living off the farm ; for if not, who else is feeding and supporting these people. But in Belgium also are great industries employing in the factories over a million men and women and drawing their supplies largely from abroad, from the Congo, from the Baltic, from Norway, from America. Belgium imports in raw material about twice the value of what she exports in raw material, and sends manufactured goods abroad to the extent of two and half times of what she buys from foreigners (17,000,000 francs against 7,000,000). The part of the population responsible for this surplus does not live off the natural resources of Belgium. Even if it consumes Belgian food, this is offset by the export surplus which it creates.

A contrasted item of calculation in the problem is found where a country exports a raw material, such as the export of coal from England or raw cotton from the United States. This item, taken in itself, would mean the potentiality of a larger population at home. But it may be offset, or more than offset, as it is in all the European industrial countries, by imports of raw material.

An extreme illustrative case is seen in the island of Java ; here 36,000,000 people live in an area of 50,000 square miles. They live in it, on it, and off it. The island is one vast plantation, feeding all its people and exporting great quantities of coffee, rubber, tobacco and tea. But its circumstances are peculiar. The island lies in the tropics, bathed in the warmth of the equatorial sea, with an exuberant soil, a dense rainfall and the luxuriant growth of a vast steaming conservatory. Not only do the people in Java maintain themselves from the resources of their territory, but undoubtedly they help to maintain, directly and indirectly, a part of the

48

population of Holland, which " owns " the island. The fact that 577 people live on each square mile of the soil gives some idea of what this globe may look like before the Malthusian night falls upon it.

From all of which it would appear that if we take single selected areas of comparison, the variation of circumstances would shut out any resulting conclusion. But we may overcome this difficulty easily if we take as the base an area sufficiently large and sufficiently varied to counteract the errors of individual cases. For this purpose I would propose to construct a " Canada in Europe " of the country lying around the Baltic Sea, the North Sea, and the English Channel. This gives us Finland, Sweden, Norway, Denmark, Germany, Holland, Belgium, the northern half of France, and the British Isles. This is a total area of 871,251 square miles. In point of latitude it lies just as Canada does from the forty-ninth parallel to the Polar Sea. East and West it extends through fifty-five meridians of longitude as compared with fifty between Montreal and Vancouver. The Gulf stream washes its western shores as the warm currents of the Pacific temper the climate of British Columbia. If the immediate basin of the Hudson Bay is rockbound, desolate and cold, the upper part of Norway, Sweden and Finland is no better. Nearly all of Norway, all from its capital Oslo upwards, lies north of all of the north-west provinces of Canada. One-third of its extent is illuminated by the midnight sun in summer and overwhelmed in the polar night in winter. Nearly all the people dwell on the coasts and along the fjords. The district of Finmark, about the size of Nova Scotia, has only

2·4 people to the square mile. Great areas in the north are without population, save a few wandering Lapps.

Of Finland, only about three per cent of the land is arable. Of the whole area of 150,000 square miles, at least one-half is unsuited for permanent habitation all the year round. The total area of the countries indicated as " *Canada in Europe* " is 871,251 square miles. They support a population of 160,000,000 people. Over so large an area it is correct to say that they are supported by the natural resources of the land and sea that they occupy. The number amounts to 184 people to the square mile. On the same basis the available area of Canada, as estimated above, can support a population of 184 to the square mile, or a total population of 250,000,000 people.

It is to be noted that this is not so much an estimate as an *under-estimate*. Where it errs it errs far on the safe side. It leaves out of count almost

Country.	Area.	Population (estimates 1925–30).
BRITISH ISLES . .	121,000	48,600,000
FRANCE (*half*) . . .	106,000	20,350,000
BELGIUM	12,000	8,000,000
HOLLAND	12,600	7,600,000
GERMANY	181,000	62,500,000
FINLAND	132,600	3,600,000
DENMARK	16,500	3,500,000
NORWAY	125,000	2,780,000
SWEDEN	173,000	6,100,000
	879,700	163,030,000

CANADA
IN EUROPE

FINLAND

NORWAY

SWEDEN

IRELAND

SCOTLAND

ENGLAND

DENMARK

HOLLAND

BELGIUM

GERMANY

FRANCE

Territory of Similar
Climate & Resources to that of Temperate Habitable
Canada. This area in Europe covers 870,700
square miles: similar territory in Canada 1,354,000 sq.
miles. This part of Europe supports over 160,000,000
people: Canada could support 250,000,000.

51

entirely vast areas, in all about a million and a half square miles, as notably the Yukon and the lower Mackenzie valley. The total estimate seems incredible. It is incredible. But it is a fact. No one in George Washington's time could have really believed that over a hundred million people would be living in the United States within the space of two lifetimes. Voltaire, when he spoke of the " acres of snow ", would have found the present city of Montreal quite incredible. The pioneers of Fort Garry, in the early 'seventies, could not have believed in the present city of Winnipeg.

Seen in this light, Canada with its 10,000,000 inhabitants appears almost empty country. So it is. Those of us who live in it do not realize this. We congregate in crowded cities and comfortable farmsteads. Our horizon is limited to the circuit of the motor-car. But those who wander and those who fly know all about it.

To fill this country with inhabitants is not a problem in individual migration. It is a vast enterprise of capital, of organization, of collective effort. Individual labour alone, however willing, could do nothing with it.

.   .   .   .

The situation of the Dominion of Canada in the British Empire is duplicated at least once on the same scale by the case of Australia : to a lesser degree in the sub-continent of South Africa (South Africa and the Rhodesias), and equally forcibly, though on a smaller scale, in the future of New Zealand and Newfoundland. It would be presumptuous for one whose knowledge of Australia,

New Zealand and South Africa is only that of a casual visitor, to endeavour to present a detailed picture of their potential development. But even the obvious facts that are accessible to all the world can show in a broad outline that in these other Dominions there is possible expansion and development of resources similar to that of Canada.

The vast area of Australia extends from the tenth to the forty-third degree of south latitude (2,000 miles). In size it is equal to four-fifths of Europe, and is as large as all the United States, without Alaska. Rather more than a third of it is within the tropics, and yet, or it would seem, on the best authority, nearly the whole of it, where it is habitable at all, is white man's country.

This is not to deny that in point of climate Australia is undoubtedly a hot place. But our ideas of the relation of climate to habitability have changed by much within the last generation or two. What was said above about the Canadian cold may be repeated in reversed terms in regard to Australian heat. The terror of the cold is mainly a question of shelter and clothing. There is no horror in a winter blizzard moving at thirty miles an hour at a temperature of thirty below zero, if you see it from the windows of a Winnipeg club. And the terrific heat of the tropics acquired its original ill omen from its connection with tropical disease, with the sudden onslaught of yellow fever or plague, which gave even death an added terror from the rapidity of its approach. The Bight of Benin and the zone of Panama are no longer death-traps to humanity.

53

Nevertheless Australia is hot. If White River in Ontario can compete for the world's crown as the coldest place on record, Wyndham on the north coast of Western Australia with an average *yearly* temperature of eighty-four and a half degrees Fahrenheit may receive the palm for heat. About two-thirds of Australia—the northern part—has an average January temperature of from eighty to eighty-five degrees and a July temperature of from fifty-five to seventy-five degrees. Even in the south and east there are terrific spells of continued heat—ninety degrees at Adelaide for a fortnight at a time, and for a week even at Sydney. There is no real winter, though there are sharp falls of temperature in Central Australia from 100 degrees by day to actual freezing-point at night. Except in the very hottest region of the northern and western coast there can be frost anywhere, and snow falls and lies on the mountains of Tasmania and the South-east. But over nearly the whole of Australia the heat is dry, and brings no inconvenience or ill-health to persons once acclimatized. Only on the north coast is the wet, saturated atmosphere scarcely bearable for Europeans in summer time. The question of a " white Australia " has long since been settled in the political sense : practically all the Australians are agreed that the continent shall be everywhere either white or empty. And in the physiological sense, while the question is still open as to the coastal region of the north, the most authoritative opinion seems to be that all the rest of Australia is white man's country. The British race certainly does not deteriorate in it—and perhaps improves.

54

But it is on rain and water, not on heat and cold, that the Australian future turns. At the present time, and indefinitely, a great part of the vast continent is withheld from human occupation for lack of water. Australia is geographically a peculiar place. It is as if one had set a huge tea tray in the southern ocean and then stamped on the centre of it so as to tip up the edge all round in a great plateau, and leave an indented centre. The edges of the plateau intercept the moist winds from the sea, the monsoons from the Indian ocean, and the south east trade winds from the Pacific, and pour them down in rain—sometimes in deluge, on the coastal rim of the continent that drops from the plateau to the sea. The centre is left dry, with nowhere enough rain and, in places, for years at a time, with none at all. About sixty-four per cent of the surface of the continent drains inward, its waters, evaporated under the fierce heat, lost in subterranean channels or swallowed in the sand. There are great "rivers", like the Darling, with a course of over 2,000 miles, which run in floods after the rain but for months are mere river-beds without water. On the map of South Australia there is marked, in flattering blue, Lake Eyre, about fifty miles wide and nearly 100 miles long. At times it is really there. At other times it is gone, and there is nothing but a stretch of mud flats, sand, scrub and barren slate. Visitors to the region assure us, however, that the presence of the Lake can always be recognized by a damp feeling in the air that blows over its bed. This great central basin of country, devoid or deficient of water, extends from South-west Queensland and the lower

" Valley of the Darling " right across the continent, in places almost to the coast. Measured north and south it has a width of about 550 miles, and this whole area represents a million square miles of territory rendered almost valueless as yet by want of water. Some years ago a distinguished scientist gave to this region the picturesque but ill-omened name, the " dead heart of Australia ", and the name has clung to it. Like most picturesque names it sacrifices truth to effect.

But if Central Australia is an arid region, conditions are entirely different in the coastal regions that lie where the central plateau falls away to the sea. Here are abundant rains, and over great areas a region of marvellous fertility where sun and soil and water combine in prodigal fertility. Rainfall in a well-watered country, such as the south of England or Western Ontario, where there is plenty of rain, never a complete drought and never a deluge, may be measured as averaging (including all precipitation of rain, snow and hail) from twenty-five to fifty inches a year. Where the rainfall sinks below ten inches a year all nature languishes, below five it lies torpid or extinct. In the Central Sahara of Africa there is no rain—never. In arid Australia an average of ten inches a year or less ; in the Lake Eyre district less than five ; in many parts of the country no rain for years at a time. But on the North-east Queensland coast there is over twelve *feet* of rain every year, and in the Australian Felix of the south-west anything from forty to sixty inches.

But the problem of the missing rain of Central Australia falls short of the grim finality of the polar cold of sub-arctic Canada. For that there is no solution. For Australia there may be. Conservation of the water during its flood rush may irrigate great areas of land now almost desert. The whole volume and fall of the water as computed for power, is not great, perhaps 1,000,000 horse-power, or about one-quarter of the available power in New Zealand and one twentieth of that in Canada. But for irrigation it can go a long way. A further hope lies in the subterranean water supply that can be reached by boring, and which gushes forth in a true "artesian" flow, or can at least be pumped to the surface. Large tracts of Queensland, New South Wales and of the north-east part of South Australia have been opened up with Artesian wells. But the whole subject is still a mystery of the future. An Artesian well *may* represent a real flow of water, drawn from higher ground, fed by surface rain and continuing for ever; or it may represent a mere sunken pocket of water urged upwards by the pressure of subterranean gasses and with a life as brief, violent and final as the soda in a siphon. Nobody knows.

But even when "arid Australia" is cast aside the rest is a wonderful land, comparable in climate, resources and possibilities to Mediterranean Europe and Northern Africa. As a pastoral country it is unsurpassed. Its sheep—even though decimated at times by recurrent droughts—number over a hundred million head. In agriculture Australia has now a wheat crop that has reached (1916) a total of 179,000,000 bushels and an annual average of about 143,000,000 ; and this though as yet not one per cent of the land of the Commonwealth is under cultivation and even in fertile Victoria only eight and a half per cent. No real estimate can be made of the arable land in Australia till the water conditions are more certain, but to say that the present total of 18,000,000 acres of cultivated land could be increased by ten to one is without doubt well within the truth.

Australia possesses vast resources of coal, placed at 165,000,000,000 tons, of which 650,000,000 is anthracite. All of the States have iron ore and plenty of it—easily accessible and workable, a total of 500,000,000 tons. In gold Australia once produced a quarter of the world's supply, even now about $10,000,000 a year. The forests of Australia cover only 38,000 square miles, or about one and one-quarter per cent of the country ; but they are predominantly of hardwood, and Australia has to import nearly half the wood required as timber. But on the other hand some of the Australian hardwood, like the jarrah and the karri of Western Australia, are of singular value for their strength and durability and are largely exported. Moreover the rapid growth of plantations of pine-trees, suitable at least for pulp, may soon create artificial forests, and the strange and mournful eucalyptus—Australia's own shadeless invention—turns out to be suited both for newsprint and for artificial silk. The parallel between Australia and the Mediterranean world may serve at least as a basis of comparison. Here are two regions of the globe with great similarity of situation and climate, with only a change of hemispheres. Each contains great stretches of desert

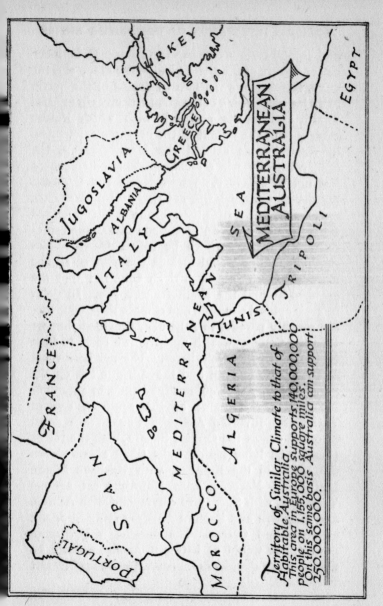

MEDITERRANEAN AUSTRALIA

Territory of Similar Climate to that of
Habitable Australia.
This area in Europe supports 140,000,000
people, on 1,155,000 square miles.
On this same basis Australia can support
250,000,000.

and coastal regions rich in vegetation. In both the softer culture of the citrous fruits, the grape and the olive, supplements the hardier grains of the north. Both lack something of the great resources in mineral wealth and forests and fish with which Nature compensates the rigours of the northern cold. And in Australia, as around the Mediterranean, the human race lives in a climate calculated to soothe but not to enervate. Where Rome and Carthage flourished, Canberra will not decline.

It would be possible therefore to construct on the same lines as the map of Canada in Europe reproduced above, a map to be called *Mediterranean Australia*. This would include the area of all the European, Asiatic and African countries that are grouped around the Mediterranean Sea. In point of geographical situation and climate these countries are roughly parallel to Australia, provided that we turn the Commonwealth upside-down so as to fit it to the northern hemispheres. The northern coast of the Mediterranean and the Adriatic lies on the parallels from 44° to 46° north latitude, or almost as far from the Equator as the southern end of Tasmania. Inverted Australia would reach down into and across the Central Sahara, with the toe of Queensland lying beside Lake Chad about eleven degrees from the Equator, with Brisbane in the latitude of Morocco, with Marseilles set against Tasmania, with Sydney to correspond with Athens, and Southern and Eastern Australia lying in Spain, in Italy and Greece. The parallel is not quite perfect. It would fit better if Australia could be moved a few degrees more from the Equator. But even as it is it offers a vivid picture of comparison, a short cut through a jungle of statistics. As with Canada so with Australia, we could begin by making a monstrous deduction of territory left out of count. We can dispense with the entire 1,000,000 square miles of " arid " Australia without prejudice to its possible future under altered conditions ; and we can throw away similarly the main desert of the Sahara and take only the countries that border round the Mediterranean Sea. This would include the whole of Portugal and Spain and the southern half of France, not used to correspond with Canada. It would take in Italy and Jugoslavia, Albania, Bulgaria and Greece ; of Turkey the European section and the Ægean littoral ; and beyond this Syria, with Egypt, the habitable parts of Italian Africa, with Tunis, Northern Algeria and Northern Morocco.

This, as the table overleaf shows, represents a total area of 1,155,300 square miles, and a population of approximately 140,000,000 people. There is no reason to believe this European and African territory in anyway superior to Australia in resources and potential support of population. If Southern France is a smiling garden it has nothing, in point of smiles, sweeter than those of the Victoria and the South Australia of the decade to come. The purple isles of the Ægean Sea are matched in the ultra-marine of Sydney harbour. A large area included on the east and south of the Mediterranean—at least 50,000 square miles—is absolutely desert. If this Mediterranean territory of a little over a million square miles maintains a population of 140,000,000,

MEDITERRANEAN AUSTRALIA

AREAS AND POPULATIONS IN ROUND NUMBERS FROM
CENSUSES AND ESTIMATES OF 1920 OR LATER

Country.	Area.	Population.
PORTUGAL	2,800	1,300,000
SPAIN	192,000	22,500,000
FRANCE (one-half) . . .	106,000	20,500,000
ITALY	120,000	41,000,000
YUGOSLAVIA.	96,000	13,000,000
ALBANIA	17,000	900,000
BULGARIA	40,000	5,700,000
GREECE	50,000	7,000,000
TURKEY (European and Ægean coast)	100,000	2,000,000
SYRIA (French)	60,000	2,000,000
PALESTINE	10,000	700,000
EGYPT (settled area only) .	13,500	14,000,000
TRIPOLI and CYRENAICA (one-half)	200,000	1,000,000
TUNISIA	50,000	2,200,000
ALGERIA (northern) . . .	80,000	5,500,000
MOROCCO (Spanish). . .	18,000	500,000
	1,155,300	139,800,000

then the 2,000,000 square miles of Australia, left
after subtracting the " dead heart ", can maintain
250,000,000.

. . . .

It is unnecessary to discuss here the great and
obvious resources of the other outer dominions—
New Zealand, South Africa and Newfoundland ; of
the huge area of the Rhodesias and Uganda, Kenya,
which may perhaps some day be the home of a

white population numbering many millions. The case speaks for itself. The assertion that half a billion inhabitants can easily be placed in the Dominions proves itself at once even on such a cursory survey as that above. Canada and Australia together could contain that number and still continue to " expand ".

Newfoundland, though too far north for real agriculture, shares with Canada in the unknown heritage of mineral wealth that now appears to lie among the rockland of the north. South Africa— vast in extent (the Union alone includes 473,089 square miles)—is still but little exploited economically. The lure of its gold turned attention away from its uncounted acres of meadow and prairie land. Its vexed history and its perplexed politics, and the dark shadow that the " native problem " casts over all Africa, has kept far from it the main stream of European, even of British migration.

New Zealand, with an area of 103,285 square miles, reproduces more closely than any other part of the Empire the climate and conditions of the mother country. Although it lies nearer to the Equator than does Great Britain, the influence of the Gulf Stream offsets the difference of latitude. Auckland is, as it were, at Land's End, with a climate to compare with that of Cornwall ; and Invercargill is " Johnny Groats ", with snow and mountains to duplicate the Highlands. New Zealand, like the mother-country, everywhere fronts the sea, and has a surface of hill and dale and varied countryside reproducing the industries, the life and the culture of Great Britain. It would seem inevitable that climate and circumstance will reproduce there the racial types of England and Scotland. If Macaulay's New Zealander of the future ever " stands upon the ruins of London Bridge ", it will be because he has the best right there.

We conclude, then, where we began, that the outer Empire can easily absorb half a billion settlers. For their coming and their increase nothing is needed but understanding of the economic problem involved. For over a hundred years mankind has been in possession of an accumulated capital and an industrial technique and a mechanism of transport adequate to the task involved. The great accumulations of industrial capital, and the monetary forms that made it fluid and usable were in full growth after the Napoleonic War. But British capital flowed all over the world and least of all to the Dominions. The flood tide stream of British migration began about 1820. But it flowed chiefly to the United States and left the Dominions empty for half a century. Transport followed in the path of capital and migration. It had not learned to go first. Only in our time have we learned that the most profitable route of a railway is to connect two places which do not yet exist.

But by our great good fortune the opportunity is still there. The gate is still open. All that is needed now is to set our minds to the way in which the expenditure of a few billion dollars can open an era of prosperity never before known.

CHAPTER III

THE HISTORICAL DEVELOPMENT OF ECONOMIC RELATIONS WITHIN THE EMPIRE

IN this chapter I propose to discuss the historical development of economic relations within the Empire. I desire to show the way in which the British colonial system became economically disarranged; how it lost through this its most illustrious colony whose inhabitants had not yet on political grounds dreamt of leaving it; how it proceeded later to imitate in a smaller degree the independence of the United States by the political separation of the responsible colonies; and how under the misleading idea of political rights the major colonies, as " Dominions " were led further and further from the benefits of economic unity until we reach the situation we have to-day. In this situation we have the spectacle of 66,500,000 British white people, united together under a single monarchy, valued by practically all of them and treasured by most of them; joined by a common language and a common literature; united by a common military glory, whose record runs unbroken from Queen Anne and Marlborough to Flanders Fields; held together by a warmth of affection and sentiment stronger than political ties; joined in

F

the casual intercourse of every day and every hour by the marvellous inventions of communication of this present era—held thus, as a unit to the wonder and envy of the world, but broken up economically into half a dozen entirely separate States without common action, or common resources or a common system of control, and unable to make use of the heritage which their history has given to them.

In this situation thus they sit, spinning fine cobwebs of discussion about their mutual political rights and glorying in their political separation.

.   .   .   .

The story of the expansion of England is too well known to require a detailed repetition. There are those who know it so well that they will prefer to turn the page ; and there are those, too, who know it so well that they are never tired of hearing it.

But I propose only briefly to review the history of the colonial empire and to do so in the light of the economic relations that were developed as between the mother country and the overseas settlements.

The British Overseas Empire begins with the island, or rather with the fisheries, of Newfoundland. Sir Humphrey Gilbert landed at what is now St. John's in 1583 and took possession of the island in the name and with the written authority of Queen Elizabeth. But the beginning was long before then. John Cabot and his son landed somewhere on the island in 1497 and claimed the whole adjacent territory—as a part of Asia—for Henry VII. The Portuguese Corte Real came three years later and announced a similar Asiatic claim. Neither explorer made any actual settlement. Neither claim had any particular meaning ; but these discoveries made known to the sailors of Western Europe the inconceivable quantities of fish at that time obtainable in the shallow waters of the Grand Banks. English, French, Portuguese and Spanish vessels came back and forward every summer. There was no attempt at settlement. The fish caught were salted and dried on the land, but the ships returned to Europe before winter. So numerous were the fish that at times the ships were unable to carry home their catch. In Queen Elizabeth's time, before Gilbert made his voyage, there were said to be some 400 vessels in the Newfoundland fishing trade. Almost a quarter of them were English.

Gilbert made his claim and was lost at sea. Others followed. An attempt was even made by Lord Baltimore, with the permission of James I, to plant a settlement. But the French worried him out of it. After that the English Government forbade all permanent settlement ; the idea was to turn the country into a sort of summer fishing station for the good of the British commercial interest. In Charles the First's time the Devon seaports alone sent 150 fishing ships to the Banks every year.

Settlements gradually followed, legal or illegal. But these were merely fishing stations. There were about 2,000 people living within the island in the days of Oliver Cromwell, and about 10,000 at the American Revolution. There was no question, as yet, of overseas migration and no real need for it. England at the opening of the Tudor times was still an undeveloped country. There were wolves in the great forests of the centre. Vast marshes extended in East Anglia, and in the north and the south-west wide and desolate moorland. Coal slumbered in its bed. The population was perhaps two and a half million. Nor for nearly 300 years after Gilbert was there any real basis for migration from over-population. Emigration when it began was not economic in its motive. It arose from persecution ; it was a means of escape ; its essence lay in its farewell. Or it was a movement of adventure, of sea-wandering, with the hope of gold and treasure ; in such cases its essence lay in the glad return. The idea of a greater England overseas had to wait for the birth of a greater England at home.

To Newfoundland followed the West Indian possessions. Beginning with Barbados (1605) a series of important islands [(Bermudas (1609) ; Bahamas (1665), etc.] were acquired by actual settlement ; one, Jamaica (1655), as a prize of war. These were " plantations " in the literal sense, a form of overseas commercial venture, to be worked with slave labour, and not constituting new homes for the people of England. These were the days when sugar filled a more important place than coal, and pepper outclassed the unknown petroleum. The spice islands of the East and West seemed like a treasure-house awaiting only the " open sesame " of European enterprise.

Of such character was the great India trading venture that began with East India Company in 1600, and reached its splendours of profit and rapacity in days of Clive. But it had nothing to do, and still has nothing to do, with the development and expansion of the British people, except through the pages of a ledger or through the annals and the arts of war. Their true homes were waiting still, away beyond the snows and over the veldt or under the sunlit shadow of the eucalyptus tree.

The first real "home" was made, and lost, in America. All the world has read the story of the Puritans of the *Mayflower* of 1620 and the Massachusetts Bay Company of 1629. They left England with a noble motive and in a good cause ; but such grief as there was at their going seems to have been one sided. Their disagreeable character was redeemed by the heroism of their endurance. They carried with them, somehow, more than any other group of outgoing emigrants, the seed of a future civilization ; the seed of American education in the people's school, a thing unknown in England ; the seed of American efficiency in their native ingenuity and smartness ; and in their code of conduct the seed of the eighteenth amendment to the constitution of the United States.

Separately came to the Virginias (1607) a people of a different kind, soon to develop great plantations, chronically half bankrupt and worked with troops of slaves hardly worth having, till the cotton gin and the English factory riveted their claims on their necks. The Virginias and such, till the Stamp Act of 1765, were further, in points of real contact, from Massachusetts than from England. Other colonies followed. Every reader of history knows of the establishment of the " towns " of Connecticut, the foundation of Rhode Island as a place where nobody

need agree with anybody ; the chartering of Pennsylvania (1681) as the home of brotherly love ; the
conquest of New York and the absorption of the
Dutch ; the broad ground plan of the Carolinas and,
last in the list, the opening (1730), of a free-for-all
refuge for the distressed named as Georgia after
George II.

Here begins in true reality the story and the
problem of the overseas British Empire. British
the provinces were, as no overseas colony ever again
except Australia and New Zealand. The emigration
was practically all from the British Isles. The
exceptions, as will be shown in the next chapter,
were so few as to leave little trace after the passage
of a generation. The migration came in waves,
proportionately of great size, at the foundation of
each colony. But after the first 100,000 of
immigrants and their offspring, the succeeding
addition was mainly by the natural increase of
population under circumstances favourable as nowhere else. Especially did migration dwindle to a
flow of small dimensions in the first half of the
eighteenth century. England could at that time
utilize its own people. Foreigners were virtually
shut out, and, in any case, did not want to come.
The cosmopolitan movement of population, irrespec-
tive of flag, allegiance and language, was still a
hundred years away. From the time when Wolfe
overcame Montcalm in 1759, the British had North
America to themselves. The Indians, in point of
numbers, never mattered. No one ever counted
them, but scholars' estimates assign perhaps one
Indian to every six square miles, not more. The

Eskimos were a legend. The French-Canadians (60,000) were agricultural prisoners of war in the St. Lawrence valley. Spanish claims mattered about as much as the Papal Bull of 1493 which defined them. Black slaves were property. There were in America, before the Revolution, 3,000,000 British people with the best continent in the world all their own : ruled, in a nominal way, by an affectionate and kindly king, no stupider than they themselves were ; deeply attached to their kindred people in the British Isles, the place which even Washington called " home ".

What a chance ! If not for humanity at large at least for all those who still spoke the common speech and shared the common history of England.

.   .   .   .

The inhabitants of the United States who are descended from Germans, Russians, or Czecho-Slovaks naturally cannot see that the American Revolution was a great tragedy. For them it was not. Without it they would probably not be there. No doubt most Americans think of the Revolution as a noble chapter in history, a great forward movement in the world's progress. Who can blame them if they do ? Such great figures as those of Washington and Jefferson, the splendid courage of the farmers and " minute men " of Bunker Hill, and the resounding phrases of the opening part of the Declaration of Independence (no one ever reads the rest) have thrown a halo around the separation of England and America.

The soil is, for many, too sacred to be treated as controversial ground. And what is more, the amaz-

71

ing material success of the United States, now rapidly tending to dominate the industrial world, seems to speak for itself. The carelessness—the superciliousness—of the English long since accepted the American Revolution as part of the general epic of British freedom, annexed George Washington as an English gentleman and agreed that the separation was inevitable. Such was the verdict of the Goldwin Smiths and the Victorian historians: a verdict which helped further to disrupt and cripple the Empire that was left after this first partition.

. . . .

But for people outside of the United States the historical problem is still worthy of attention. And most of all to us who live in Canada, whose past history, whose present situation and whose whole future are intimately concerned.

. . . .

The truth is, that the American Colonies were not separated from England because of political discontent. There wasn't enough of it to notice. The colonies governed themselves. The great mass of the people, ninety-nine out of every hundred, never dreamed of independence. No one, so Benjamin Franklin has assured us, ever dreamed of independence before 1775, whether drunk or sober. Washington repudiated the very idea of it as late as the year 1775. There were, in colonial days, no conspiracies, no underground plots, no patriots taking oaths in a cellar at midnight, no Catilines, no Guido Fawkes—nothing. All the quarrel that there was was focused in the decade from 1765 to 1775, and it rested on economic grounds, not political.

The quarrel led to actual fighting, Lexington was only a skirmish, yet Bunker Hill was a fierce and appalling conflict with a British loss of over a thousand dead and wounded, not far from twice as many as the British killed, wounded and missing (655) of the battle on the Plains of Abraham, sixteen years before.

Fighting such as this leads to war. A declaration of war only followed twelve months after Bunker Hill, under the name of the Declaration of Independence. According to the words of this document, the separation that followed was mainly based on inalienable political rights and the rejection of political tyranny. But nobody, except here and there an Adams and a Patrick Henry, had ever thought of this before. One may find such people to-day here and there in Canada, or even in New Zealand, talking school-book republicanism. But nobody pays any more attention to them than the American at large did to Samuel Adams before the summer of 1775.

．　．　．　．　．　．　．　．

But the economic situation is worth studying.

The old colonial system regulating the relations of the plantations to the mother-country in the eighteenth century, like many other things, was not as black as it has been painted. In its essential basis it was far ahead of what we have now, for it started from the idea of the unity of all the British possessions, whereas we start now, since 1840, with the idea of their separation. The old colonial system regarded all foreign countries as on a different footing from the British Empire. Our present regime—

save for a few preferential gestures—treats all parts of the Empire as countries, foreign to one another. The colonial system contained in itself the idea of a distinct purpose, namely British Unity—which it failed to achieve. The present system is stamped equally plainly with the idea of ultimate separation, which may yet be prevented.

The colonial system began with the idea that all the land in all British possessions belonged to the Crown, meaning the Imperial Government in Great Britain. This was excellent. It compares admirably with the present silly notion that 600,000 settlers in Alberta, by a new arrangement of 1930, are the uncontrolled owners of 100,000,000 acres of unoccupied fertile land ; that the 333,000 people lost in the 975,000 square miles of Western Australia own every foot of it. Who else in the early days of settlement should own the enormous and unknown territory, on the edges and outskirts of which a few new-comers have clustered, except the government from which they come, whose flag and arms still shelter them ? The premature abandonment of the imperial ownership of unused lands was one of the most disastrous errors of colonial policy.

It is true that in colonial days the grants were often enormous in extent and foolish in lavish generosity to the undeserving. But often they were not. William Penn received 45,000 square miles to manage as a proprietor under the Crown and Parliament—perhaps the best disposition ever made of colonial land. As the colonies grew, the royal governors on the spot, as in Virginia, made grants of land to individual settlers, a practice that lasted far into the nineteenth century. But behind this power of the governor was still, quite properly, the over-riding authority of the Crown. When the colonies undertook to grant to the Ohio Company and such the lands beyond the Alleghany mountains, unsurveyed and empty, the Crown interfered. This vast territory was not to belong to the 3,000,000 people who happened to get to America first. The unoccupied land of the Empire, apart from actual settlements, from land reclaimed with the axe and defended with the musket, was Royal Domain. Substitute for " royal " the word " British " and the proposition ought to hold good to-day. It did hold good till well into the nineteenth century. This ownership of the public land by the Imperial Government proved the means of settlement for the United Empire Loyalists. The system finished with responsible government. What was done cannot be undone. It is a clock that we cannot turn back. But we can at least realize the economic check involved in the transfer of vast areas of land to the mimic ownership of a few settlers.

In the colonial days, however, no one thought much about the question of the land. There seemed so much of it. George Washington, by inheritance and marriage, by purchase and speculation, acquired some 100,000 acres. No one worried over this. In the gorgeous and bountiful endowment in which even the humblest American lived, there was no room for a land question.

More complicated was the control of commerce. The British Government expected the plantations to be a source of profit to the commercial interest of

Great Britain. Hence arose the mercantile code which presented to the other country the whole colonial market to sell in, and the whole colonial export in such great articles as tobacco and sugar. But even this was not quite as one sided as it seemed. Colonial tobacco, for instance, had a virtual monopoly of the English market. Home growing was very early prohibited. The colonies also could trade with one another to the exclusion of the foreigners. The United States realized this at once, when their independence of 1783 shut them out of the West Indian market.

The British Government, as a matter of British interest, fully intended the colonies to flourish, especially the West Indies and such, true " plantations ", enterprises of investment, as opposed to Massachusetts and New England at first deservedly and desiredly disregarded.

Manufacture, except the domestic handicraft of the farm, the forge and the loom, was denied. A resolution of the House of Commons in 1719 declared " that the erecting of manufactures in the colonies tended to lessen their dependence upon Great Britain ". The sentiment was crudely, even brutally expressed ; but the real idea is excellent. Substitute " union " for " dependence " and the resolution becomes almost a caress. Truly excellent was the shipping and navigation code, the visible result of which, down the decades, is the British mercantile marine of to-day. Everybody has heard of the Navigation Acts that dominated English policy in the mercantile days and only finally passed away in 1849. Such statutes have their origin as far back as the reign of Richard II, but it is the series of statutes of Charles II (1660, 1661, 1663 and 1672) which constituted the famous code for the regulation of the colonial trade. Their general purpose was to keep English trade in English ships, built in England, officered by Englishmen and manned with at least three Englishmen to every four of the crew. It accepted a measurable economic loss for a political and national gain of incalculable extent. The Acts went further and regulated the substance of trade. The great staple colonial articles—sugar, tobacco, cotton-wool and others could only be carried to English territory. Foreigners were forbidden to be merchants in the colonies, and, a more doubtful provision, duties were levied on goods shipped from colony to colony.

The Navigation Acts interfered with natural liberty at every point. Yet even Adam Smith couldn't find it in his heart to condemn them. " Defence ", he said, expressing himself with unaccustomed brevity, " is better than opulence." In point of fact the laws were tempered with exceptions and exercised at the colonial ports with a salutary negligence. Much important trade was left open. New England could send its fish direct to Catholic Europe. The trade in grain was unimpeded, the trade in timber and rum was positively encouraged.

The whole code of colonial regulation was awkward, unsystematic, and here and there vexatious. But on the whole it could have been fashioned true imperial system. It was the attempt to add to it the burden of taxation that broke the system down. England was appalled by the growth of the national debt, which was mistaken by the ignorance of the eighteenth century for national indebtedness. The Stuart kings never had a debt except in and out of their pocket. They hadn't the credit. The national debt originated (1694) with banking and the expansion of national wealth and the creation of credit mechanism. That it could exist at all was a sign of a national stability never known before. But its bearing was not understood, and its rapid increase aroused misgivings. After the French War (1756–63) the debt stood at £132,000,000. (In 1928 it stood at £7,631,000,000.) This was alarming. England undertook by means of the Stamp Act of 1765, and the new customs acts (tea, etc.) which followed it, to collect a revenue to offset the cost of American defence. This led to controversy, to anger, to rioting, then to " petition-ing in arms ", to rebellion and finally to independ-ence. The old colonial system ended in the disastrous separation of 1783.

. . . .

Having lost one colonial empire England set to work in a queer haphazard way to make another. The settlement of the peace of 1783 occasioned the migration of the Loyalists and necessitated the establishment of Australia. The United Empire Loyalists, refusing to remain in the new American republic, were moved at the expense of the British Government to Nova Scotia (1783–1799) and into Upper Canada. Some of them came because they dared no longer stay at home, but for the most part they were people of patriotism, energy and substance, whose history soon proved their real worth. The economic circumstances of their settlement are of great interest for the present discussion. It shows what could be done now on a scale vastly greater and with equal success. With aid in transport, money and land from the accumulated capital of Great Britain over 40,000 Loyalists were transported. The operation was enormously successful and profitable. It has returned a fabulous, if incalculable, interest. In a later chapter the circumstances of the settlement will be further examined. But we note it here historically chiefly to regret that the movement of migration came to so early an end. There was no need to limit to it the " Loyalists " of New York and Massachusetts. Every pauper in England was a " loyalist " ; every dispossessed weaver among the victims of the power loom was a " loyalist " ; the unhappy children of the parish carried round by the cartful and sold as pauper apprentices for the new factories, all these were " loyalists ". If in these and the succeeding decades, when English capital went to bolster up rickety Greek Governments, to build Erie canals and buy Pennsylvania bonds—if there had only been the knowledge of how to use it !

.   .   .   .

Then came Australia. Its existence as a legend goes back to ancient times. The Dutch had touched its shores early in the seventeenth century. English sailors had seen it from Dampier's ship in 1688. But no one claimed it. No one wanted it. The world of the seventeenth century was still inconceivably vast, and few foresaw how rapidly it would shrink to the little globe on which we live. British ownership begins with Captain James Cook's voyage to the South Seas of 1768–70, undertaken to allow a group of Royal Society astronomers to view the transit of Venus. Cook circumnavigated New Zealand and sailed along the south-east coast of Australia. From a fancied resemblance to a more familiar shore he named it New South Wales. Cook claimed the land, found a wonderful bay where "great quantity of plants" grew and named it Botany Bay. The report made by Captain Cook and his companions was favourable, even enthusiastic. The Government determined to take up the claim. It seemed necessary. The American colonies had served among other purposes as a place for the transportation of criminals. After independence began, the United States had no need, has never since had any need, to import foreign criminals. The colonization began, as all the world knows, with the expedition of 1787–88 in which Captain Arthur Phillip and a fleet of eleven vessels landed at Botany Bay 717 "criminals", both men and women, convicted of all sorts of offences, great and small, real and imaginary. Within a short time the discovery of the marvellous grazing land behind the barrier of inaccesible mountains that shut in the convict settlement, changed the whole character of the colony. Within a generation, a quarter of a million sheep were grazing on the Bathurst plains. A few free settlers had come in within three or four years of Phillip's landing. But for three decades the colony was mainly made up of "emancipated" convicts. Even in 1821 the "emancipists" and their families numbered over 13,000 as against 2,500 free settlers. But the migration after the Napoleonic War soon washed out the convict stain.

Thus, by one of the marvels of British good fortune, was secured, unopposed and unquestioned, the control of a continent.

The outcome of the same wars brought with the settlement of 1815 a great accretion of territory to the British Crown. The Cape of Good Hope (276,995 square miles) and Ceylon (25,481 square miles) taken from the Dutch during their eclipse as the Batavian Republic, and with these, Trinidad and Malta, British Guiana, the Seychelles and Mauritius. The opportunity was now open to found again a British Empire in permanent unity and strength. Unfortunately the drift of Fate was against it. The current of opinion and events during the next generation bore on its surface, not the materials for making a new British Empire but for making a whole series of New United States.

From the outbreak of the French War in 1793 till the final peace of 1815, colonial policy was entirely dominated by the exigencies of the military and naval situation. But even before the war a powerful set of forces of an entirely new character was coming into being, and was destined presently to alter the entire outlook. The improvements in the processes of production in the eighteenth century, the utilization of coal, the application of steam and water-power, the consequent creation of factory industry in the place of house industry, the cheapening of transportation by improved roads and by canals, had brought about what has since been called the industrial revolution.

Central and Northern England changed from a land of great estates to a land of factory workshops, of coal mines, of iron or steel. Commerce multiplied at the sea ports of the " workshop of the world ", now easily first, and long without even a second. New interests began to dictate a new policy, a world policy in place of the insular mercantilism of the preceding centuries. And mingling with the roar of the new machines could be heard already, as an undertone, the first murmurings of a self-conscious working class. The theoretical basis of this new and cosmopolitan outlook had been laid even before the French War, was in the writings of Hume and the French " Economists ", and, above all, by Adam Smith. But Smith's *Wealth of Nations*, which was meant to teach, among other things, the art of retaining the American colonies, was not published till the year 1776, when they were already lost.

It remained for the powerful commercial interests of Manchester and Birmingham and other manufacturing centres to force into practical legislation the policy of the *laissez-faire* inspired by the theories of Smith. After the Napoleonic wars, the manufacturers of England had no more need of protection. The demand arose for the removal of all duties, whether on manufactures or on raw material or on food. This demand, rising into a great national movement and taking to itself, under the inspired leadership of Cobden and Bright, something of the aspects of a religious crusade, attained its overwhelming triumph in the spectacular repeal of the duties on corn in 1846 and the destruction (1842–63) of the whole protective system. The economic aspects of free trade fall into the discussion of a later chapter. But it is to be noted here that " free trade "—the abolition of protective duties— was only one aspect of the system and programme of " national liberty ". It involved also the removal of governmental regulation of industry, of laws of apprentices (1813), of laws of settlement, the establishment of freedom of combination for workmen (1824–5), and the removal, presently (1849), of what was left of the navigation laws.

Most of all, it affected the economics of colonial policy. The British Colonial Empire that sprang up after 1783 was governed much as had been the lost empire of the thirteen American provinces. The British Government regulated the customs duties by imperial acts ; it maintained in modified shape the navigation laws ; it granted lands ; it maintained garrisons ; it regulated all shipping. But it gave to these colonists political privileges equal to those that the Americans had enjoyed. An elected provincial assembly had been set up in Halifax in 1758 as the official expression of an existing right of Britons overseas ; in New Brunswick in 1784 ; in Upper and Lower Canada in 1791 after the Loyalists moved in ; and in New South Wales in 1842 ; in Queensland, Victoria, South Australia, Tasmania and New Zealand shortly after.

But the situation contained within itself the making of its own ruin. It was neither one thing nor the other ; it was not economic unity under central control and it was not economic separation under independence. After its first settlement of the Loyalists the British Government did little to develop any of the Dominions. The fatal idea that everything developed itself, if let alone, paralysed action. The accumulation of pecuniary capital which now began to form in what had become the money market of London, flew away in this and that direction : it went into foreign loans, American canal securities and South American revolutions. Little of it went to the undeveloped colonies. There was no understanding of what to do. England had men to throw away, paupers to deplore, money to invest and new apparatus of steam and machinery to give it power. But the dominant notion of the time was to leave it all alone, to follow the line of least resistance. England followed it. Meantime the "liberated" United States of America, with economic unity of control and economic power over resources, were witnessing an onrush of material development, easily mistaken for a consequence of political independence.

.   .   .   .

The trouble that was bound to come in such a case to all the colonies, came first to the two Canadas. They were the largest in population, 427,000 in Lower Canada in 1822, in Upper Canada 150,000 in 1824, while as yet even in New South Wales the population was only 35,000 in 1828. The Loyalists of Canada, moreover, had within sight across the St. Lawrence and across Lakes Ontario and Erie, the aspect of American prosperity to contrast with their own stagnation.

The fact that in Lower Canada five people out of

every six were French complicated the situation
and added national rancour to political discontent.
There followed the abortive double rebellion of
1837–8, an event local and even insignificant in
its occurrence, but world-wide in its consequences.
The change of government that followed in the
Canadas, and was afterwards extended all over the
British Empire, has become one of the great factors
in the world's present outlook. Lord Durham, as
everybody knows, came out to Canada in 1838 as
High Commissioner to find out how the rebellion
had arisen. He finds its cause in the lack of political
freedom and in the struggle of two nations " warring
in the bosom of a single state ". He recommended
as the cure for it that the colonies should receive
" responsible government " ; this would satisfy all
just and proper demands of the British malcontents,
of which Lord Durham as an advanced Whig
thoroughly approved ; and this—by combining at
the same time the government of the Upper and the
Lower Province into a single legislature—would vote
out of existence the French and terminate their
" vain hope of nationality ", and the survival of
their language : a culmination of which Lord Durham as a thorough Englishman warmly approved.
Such was the measure of Lord Durham's foresight.

Responsible government—after a little subsequent
bickering as to its application—came with the Act
of 1840 which united the two Canadas. At the
same time it was extended to Nova Scotia and to
New Brunswick ; and by parity of reasoning to
New South Wales, New Zealand and the other
Australian colonies (1854–6). It was extended

similarly to the Cape Colony in 1872 and Natal in 1893. Its application to the Transvaal and to the Orange Free State in 1906 rests in an entirely other setting. In the colonies of the middle century it foreshadowed an independence to come. For the Transvaal and the Free State it replaced an independence that was lost. There is no connection between the two. One act was an error in statesmanship, the other a glorious triumph.

.   .   .   .

The grant of political self-government to the greater colonies in the middle century was accompanied by a loosening, indeed a casting off, of all economic ties. After 1846 England permitted the self-governing colonies to frame their own tariffs. The final repeal of the Navigation Acts in 1849 left them in control of their own shipping. The public lands went to the new Dominions in full and complete sovereignty. Between the event of the Canadian rebellion of 1837 and the confederation of the Dominion of Canada there elapsed thirty years, one generation. In this time the whole aspect of the Empire was altered. It became and remained a group of economically independent States.

This movement of disruption was greeted at the time with self-complacent satisfaction. It was another triumph of the idea of natural liberty, of *laissez-faire*, of enlightened self-interest, which appeared to have done so much already for national wealth and progress in England. Few voices were raised in protest. Only here and there was doubt expressed about handing over to the miniature civilization of the colonies the vast heritage of land

and resources which they could neither occupy, utilize or defend. Only a few realized that the regime of *laissez-faire* was only a passing phase, only a chapter in the economic history of Great Britain. Here and there was heard a voice in the wilderness. " Self-government ", said Disraeli in 1872, looking back on the irremediable, " ought to have been conceded as part of a great policy of imperial consolidation. It ought to have been accompanied by an Imperial tariff, and by securities for the people of England for the enjoyment of unappropriated lands." Quite so. But the harm had already been done. The climax had already been reached when the whole vast area of North-west Canada was separated from British control (existing through the overlordship of the Hudson's Bay Company) and given to the new Dominion of Canada. It took the people of Canada almost twenty years to build a Pacific Railway—a creditable and courageous enterprise for such a minor population with so little wealth. But Great Britain could have built it in a couple of years. The United States had already built five.

There was some protest, also, in certain quarters, when the colonies used their new liberty to set up protective tariffs against England. This was done in the province of Canada in 1859 to respond to the rising demands of local manufacturers. In England certain bodies such as the Chamber of Commerce of Sheffield petitioned the Imperial Government to act. But the Government disclaimed all constitutional power. It reasserted this again in 1887 when the effect of the protective tariff of the Dominion (the National Policy of 1879) began to be felt in the mother-country. Meantime, the colony of Victoria, where severe local unemployment was crying out for a remedy, had followed Canada's lead in adopting against England, as well as the outside world, the protective tariff, since then a permanent feature of Australian policy.

Looking back now, it is hard to believe that the statesmen of the Empire could so deliberately have broken it up. The explanation lies in the background of the scene. It was not merely that the leading minds of the period did not foresee what would happen. The trouble was that they foresaw a lot of things that didn't happen. They foresaw universal free trade, a matter for them of simple common sense. The trade of every nation would be open to every other. " Ownership " and control of colonies would have no meaning. There was nothing in the economic world but individual work and individual interest : national well-being was merely the sum total of all this. There was no need for regulation, for state action, for legislation : all of this was as antiquated as the mediæval guild. This dream of a cosmopolitan world was, and is, as beautiful a picture as ever brightened the horizon of hope. At some distant day humanity may yet find it at the end of the rainbow.

. . . .

In the last quarter of the nineteenth century, as all the world knows, the pendulum swung the other way. Free trade, even as an aspiration, except in Great Britain and New South Wales, faded out. War took the place of peace. The new industrial power looked about for new materials and new markets. Asia and Africa were divided up. Imperialism began again.

England got its full share of the partition in such vast additions as Nigeria, East Africa, the Rhodesias, in all a total of about a million and a half square miles and a population of new native subjects to the extent of 30,000,000.

But Imperialism in the sense of complete economic union with the Dominions was no longer possible. The basis was gone. An Imperial Federation League sprang up over night into a mushroom growth (1884), but perished under the cold breath of colonial suspicion abroad and Cobdenite indifference at home. The conferences—colonial (1887, 1897, 1902) and later imperial (from 1907)—began to work out a form of permanent union by means of permanent separation. Meantime for all the Dominions each separate thread of political connection was worn thin and then snapped asunder. Till the middle of the nineteenth century British military garrisons still guarded the colonies. They were withdrawn— from Canada in 1862, then from Australia and New Zealand, and one by one from all the Dominions. United naval defence lingered on till England tired of paying for it without help. The naval establishments at Halifax and Esquimalt were terminated in 1909–10. The Imperial Australasian squadron was exchanged for an Australian fleet. In vain the Admiralty, in a swan-song called the Memorandum of 1902, preached the strategy of united defence. It was too late. After that, only war could unite it.

Link by link was broken. Justice lingered. The

Crown pardoned, or refused to pardon, criminals till 1878. A representation from the Canadian Department of Justice altered the situation ; after that, the Dominion claimed the right to hang its own. The final appeal to the King's Privy Council —historically the last right of the subject to throw himself at the King's feet—lingers still, but apparently only through the favour of the lawyers. Even at that, Australia limits it, and the Free State, it seems, with a strange home-sickness for something to rebel at, is prepared to circumvent all effects of the appeal in liberated Ireland.

Even the diplomatic unity of the Empire in dealing with foreign Powers is ended. By a series of gradations beginning with Lord Elgin's treaty with the United States in 1854 and ending with the Halibut treaty of 1923, the Dominions have acquired, bit by bit, the right to make their own treaties. If these stages were meant as footsteps towards independence, they were excellent. If not, each step led out further into the wilderness.

The Great War threw into a high light the wonderful kinship in spirit of all the British peoples. History has never witnessed such a united front. But the war, by showing that combined defence was still possible and successful without political union, encouraged rather than impeded the process of breaking away. Six great Dominions became members of the League of Nations. Apart from the all-embracing bond of the Crown and a common allegiance, and apart from the lawyers' haven of the Privy Council, it became hard to see in what way the British Empire is a political empire at all. The relation between its parts has become a sort of riddle of the sphinx. There is no answer.

From the Press and the platform, the Parliament and the college debating society, pours an endless discussion as to where and what we are in our political relations to each other. All needless. This discussion, if it goes on, will crystallize into something as interesting as the Chinese classics—and about as useful. The point of interest, the question of importance, the means of salvation for the British Empire no longer lies in the political relations of its parts. Self-government, autonomy, has come. It is there to stay. It is an accepted fact. As to the difference between autonomy and independence that is a mere riddle of the sphinx, of practical interest to no one but the writers of textbooks. The great questions of our future—the question of bread and work and happiness for all—lie elsewhere and must look in other directions for a settlement.

CHAPTER IV

THE MIGRATION OF POPULATION IN THE PAST

IT ought to be possible to set up a movement of population and capital on a vast scale to develop the unoccupied land and the unused resources of the British Empire. This should not be a movement of little groups, of unaided pioneers and single settlers. It should be a matter of millions of men and billions of money. It can be done.

If successful, such a movement would give free rein, for many generations to come, to the natural increase in British stock. It would banish unemployment as with the wave of a wand. It would, for many generations to come, give to every one concerned a real opportunity in life, bread and work for all, and success everywhere for those of steadfast industry and purpose. This is all that honest people can ask.

The thing can be done. It must be possible. The evidence lies in the fact that every economic element needed is waiting to be put into its place. Two centuries ago, in the old colonial days, such a thing was not possible. Accumulated capital was but small. The machine had not yet come. Transport was still primitive. Nature was still unconquered. Now all is changed. The accumulated capital needed to move a million people across an ocean, and establish homes for them, is a mere nothing compared to the vast total of capital in existence. In point of transport the whole operation could be organized by any competent traffic official in one afternoon. And the population is waiting : without drawing on alien sources at all, we could bring at once 2,000,000 people from Great Britain to the Dominions, and soon find, with a full natural increase of population, 2,000,000 more to follow every year.

One can, in imagination at least, form a picture of such a great outgoing tide, moving noiselessly and without effort or struggle. The labour of those who come, applied to new land and resource, supplies the surplus that brings still more. The immigrant population, if properly varied, is its own support. It supplies its own market. It works its own salvation.

Yet contrast such a picture of continuous and prosperous settlement with what has happened in the past. There were first the isolated days of pioneer settlement, a hand-to-hand struggle ; capital was utterly lacking ; machines were unknown ; numbers were too few for associated toil on any large scale. Hunger and want were but at arm's length. Death took its toll everywhere. Of the Pilgrim settlers of 1620 one-half by the end of the first winter were buried on Cole's hill, the graves laid flat and without headstones so as to conceal their death from the knowledge of the savages. Some settlements, like that of the Huguenots in Florida, vanished off the earth. Others narrowly escaped. In the infant settlement of Virginia (1622) no less than 350 persons were massacred by the Indians, and of the rest, disease and famine removed fifty per cent before relief came to them. Even in the nineteenth century Lord Selkirk's colonists, moving into what is now one of the granaries and gardens of the world, could barely survive. Decimated by the fevers that haunted the crowded emigrant ships, slaughtered by enemies and their substance devoured for years (1818 and onwards) by great flocks of locusts against which they had nothing to avail, they almost disappeared from the earth. Later on, while technique and capital should have made genuine migration possible, there followed an era of wild rushes into new country, of a temporary " boom " of prosperity, as in Manitoba and South Australia, followed by sudden and disastrous collapse. And in our own time we reach a condition of stalemate—a deadlock —with landless people on one side of the ocean and empty land on the other.

But to understand the migration problem of the present, the best way is to examine the migration of the past—its circumstances and conditions, its few conspicuous successes and the warning of its innumerable failures.

. . . .

Let us begin a long way back.

In the fourteenth century, England, where it did not consist of forests and fen, of marsh and moorland, was an agricultural country of about 4,000,000 inhabitants. Then came the great plague of 1349, the Black Death. It destroyed nearly half the

people, leaving perhaps two millions and a half.
Recovery was slow. For over a hundred years there
was no growth. Even at the opening of the Tudor
century the population is only estimated at
3,000,000. But there followed a period of great
economic change. Society was disintegrated by
the break-up of the monastic lands ; by the eviction
of the small peasantry in favour of pasture-making ;
by the continuous rise in prices that followed the
advancing wave of Spanish gold. All this broke
the mould in which mediæval society was cast.
Population grew apace and without adequate means
of support. There appeared a flock of beggars,
vagrants, idle and lawless men. This caused alarm.
It was thought that England must get rid of them.
Sir Humphrey Gilbert spoke of the " needy people
of the country who now trouble the Commonwealth ". Richard Hakluyt, the famous compiler
of the *Voyages*, speaks of the vagrants " who go
up and down in swarms for lack of honest entertainment ".

These tears and laments were really groundless.
The over-population was apparent, not real. The
resources of England itself were still undeveloped.
But it was these groundless apprehensions which
helped to set in motion the first wave of migration
toward North America. These fears also gave a
false bias to British emigration which has lasted
until our time. It was a policy of " casting out " :
its results were seen for two centuries in the stream
of indentured criminals and paupers banished to
America, of convicts carried to Australia, and
pauper children shipped to anywhere or nowhere.

Other motives joined. Most of the Puritans were religious refugees. Many of the Virginians were adventurers. The West Indians—on a great scale or a small—planter capitalists.

The stream ran strongly from the accession of James I to the end of the century of the Stuarts, from the Virginia establishment of 1607 and the *Mayflower* of 1620 till the opening of the eighteenth century. In the reign of Queen Anne (1700) the population of England had risen to five and a half million, but there was now no over-population. The rise of home industry and commerce held it in check for another hundred years. Meantime, to the West Indies there had gone a British population which, in 1700, with its increase on the spot, reached 50,000. But with it were now 100,000 negro slaves. The introduction of the negroes checked wherever it fell the movement of white labour. In Jamaica there were put, in spite of fevers and hardships, during the regime of the Commonwealth which had captured it, 4,000 whites and 1,000 negroes. A quarter of a century later the negroes had been increased by ten to one, the white only by two to one. Migration to the North American provinces of Great Britain in the seventeenth century was almost entirely British. There were a few exceptions. The conquest of New Amsterdam (New York) in 1664 incorporated some 7,500 Dutch, a mere leaven in the lump, albeit a strengthening one. The outcast Huguenots, after 1685, looked for new homes. A few came to Massachusetts and to New York, a good many (500 in one body in the year 1700) to the South. But their language rapidly faded out, and even their names were either translated or mispronounced to extinction.

A more notable exception was found in the coming of the " Pennsylvania Dutch ", Germans from the Palatinate, who left Europe after the ravages of Marlborough's campaigns. The British Government planted nearly 10,000 of them in Pennsylvania in Queen Anne's time, and other bodies followed in groups from then till the close of the colonial period. These people kept their language and remained a distinctive element in the population, miscalled " Dutch " through the linguistic ignorance of their fellow-citizens. But migration, as a whole, slackened after the close of Queen Anne's war. Industry was increasing and the era of iron and coal was dawning. There was work at home. As a result there was no general plan or scheme of emigration, except for the criminal class. These were carried over by contract and sold into service for seven or fourteen years. This helped to check the emigration of free men, a check that was further emphasized by the slave ship and its cargo of negro slaves. For the period 1680 to 1786 the total number of negro slaves introduced into the British colonies was 2,130,000, or an annual import of 20,000. The greater part went to the thirteen colonies. At the first census the ex-slaves and their offspring numbered 757,000.

But if free immigrants were thus shut out from contract labour in the plantation States they could have land for the asking. There was plenty everywhere.

It followed, therefore, from what has been said

that the white population of the American colonies in the colonial days was almost entirely native born. Migration had been replaced by natural increase. Families grew fast, children, in the rural parts, at least—and almost all America was rural—were a blessing and an asset. A widow with a growing family was a matrimonial prize. Benjamin Franklin was one of a flock of seventeen. It was Franklin himself who calculated that in America population was doubling every twenty-five years. Under these circumstances minor foreign elements of language and culture washed easily out. The Swedes of Delaware left no trace ; even the Dutch of Manhattan and the Hudson very little, except in point of sentiment and pride. The country was all British at the time of the conquest of Canada, more so than Canada itself has ever been, and comparable in this aspect to the Australia and New Zealand of to-day.

Its British character was heightened during the last generation of the colonial life by the tide of migration that set in during the period between the conquest of Canada and the outbreak of the American Revolution. The rebellion of 1745, the break-up of the clans and the economic poverty of the Highlands and of Ireland, set in movement the most serious volume of migration that had gone forth since the original establishment of the colonies. It has been estimated that 40,000 Ulster-Scots left the northern ports of Ireland in the five years before the summons of the Continental Congress. From the lochs and harbours of north-west Scotland ship-loads of Highlanders set forth for the Carolinas or for the King's newly organized province of Nova Scotia.

. . . .

The close of the American Revolution brought with it the most important, the most significant episode in the story of British migration—the transfer of the Loyalists to what is now Canada. What happened has an important bearing on the situation of to-day. The transfer was a huge success. At a relatively small cost—though the sacrifice seemed large at the time—it set up a British community in a new and fertile territory, whose wealth has since returned a thousand times all that was spent on the undertaking.

In all, some 40,000 Loyalists were moved into British North America. In the year immediately following the war (1784) about 25,000 were settled in Prince Edward Island, Nova Scotia and the western section of Nova Scotia organized as New Brunswick. Other Loyalists migrated by way of the Hudson and Lake Champlain to the southern part of what is now Quebec (the Eastern townships), left relatively empty by the French settlers who had preferred to string out along the St. Lawrence and the Richelieu. Others went down the Richelieu to Sorel, wintered there and then made their way up the St. Lawrence to Lake Ontario. And others again moved west through the forests of New York State and so to the Niagara River and Lake Ontario. The transit was arduous. There were no roads, no shelter by the way, no food except that carried. To-day the 30,000 Loyalists who thus came to Upper Canada could all have run over in their motor-cars in one morning and back (if on the quota) in the afternoon. *Tempora mutantur*. A century and a half ago the infiltration lasted several years. The British Government stood behind it. It supplied transport where it could. It handed out rations of food for some three years. It gave land, the original grant being on the scale of 2,000 to 5,000 acres for officers, 200 acres for non-commissioned officers, and 100 each for the men. Some Loyalists came in compact lots or units, like the Highlanders from western New York, who were settled along the upper St. Lawrence (1784) and followed other groups of Highlanders from Scotland, including (1802) the Glengarry Fencible Regiment, who gave the name to the district. For those who had lost homes and property by confiscation in the United States, the Government paid money; £4,000,000 was spent on this.

.   .   .   .

Here was a real beginning of a consolidated Empire. All that was needed was to continue on the lines indicated by the Loyalist settlement. But the spirit of the time was against it. The Napoleonic wars impeded and almost terminated migration till after the peace of 1815. In the period which followed, the dominant conception of *laissez-faire* left the movement of capital and the outflow of population chiefly under the direction of individual incentive. Within a very short time individual incentive guided both the capital and the settlers in directions other than British.

.   .   .   .

In the period between the peace treaty of 1815

and the beginning of responsible government in the colonies the British Government indeed did something towards systematic colonization. Imperial authority still controlled the public land, and the Imperial Government had therefore a legislative power over colonization never since possessed. Moreover, the war of 1812 had seemed to emphasize the need of a "loyal" population in the Canadas for defence against the United States. Considerations of Imperial defence have always moved the British Government more readily to action than any other reasons of policy. As a consequence a number of transfers of emigrant colonies were managed, directly and indirectly by the Home Government. In 1815 and 1816 about fourteen hundred settlers were carried free to Upper Canada, placed on the land, with 100 acres for each family, and supplied with a temporary loan of money. The plan was not continued. But various group settlements were made with government aid in the period between this time and the Canadian rebellion of 1837—in the Rice Lake district, in the county of Lanark and elsewhere. In 1821 the Imperial Government granted £68,000 to aid Irish immigration. Irish colonies were brought out, under the direction of Peter Robinson (whose name lingers in the town of Peterboro'), in the years 1823 and 1825. In all, some 5,000 people were established.

To these exertions of the Government, private efforts were added. Thomas Douglas, Lord Selkirk, had already distinguished himself as a pioneer of Empire. At a time when the great "clearances" in the Highlands were turning out the peasantry to make way for the sheep, Selkirk had brought (1803) three shiploads, 800 people, to Prince Edward Island. Encouraged by this, he obtained a grant of land of 110,000 acres on the Red River, and from then until his death laboured unceasingly to promote an agricultural colony in the North-west. Commercial jealousy, faction, violence, and lack of capital virtually ruined Selkirk's plans and laid him in the grave at the age of forty-eight. His aim had been to make the west of Canada something better than a buffalo pasture and a beaver meadow. The truth was buried with him for half a century, while the buffalo wallowed in Alberta and the British settlers moved into Kansas.

More successful was Colonel Talbot, a veteran of the Revolutionary War, who first came to Upper Canada with Governor Simcoe and returned about ten years later to help colonize the Lake Erie district. Talbot received 5,000 acres from the Government, and settled twenty townships, each settler receiving fifty acres. The plan was overwhelmingly successful.

To this was added the operation of the land companies. The Canada Land Company was founded in 1824 by John Galt, a brilliant and energetic Scotsman whose plan for the development of the colony was based on that happy blending of public activity and private enterprise which is the true secret of colonization. Galt raised money in England for the purchase of land from the Government at the rate of about £20,000 a year. The land bought by the company included almost two and a half million acres. It embraced a part of the western peninsula of Ontario and a tract on the shores of Lake Huron. Nearly all was unbroken forest. The Government accepted the building of roads, bridges, churches and schools as part payment on the price. Public spirit and shrewd commercial sense were combined in true Scottish fashion. " The objects of the company," so it was stated in the Journals of the Assembly of Upper Canada, " will be to purchase waste and uncleared land in this province, and to settle, clear and dispose of such land, together with the subsidiary objects of making advances of capital to settlers, opening and improving roads and other internal communications, and promoting the cultivation of such articles as can advantageously be exported from the province." There was a certain nobility in the enterprise, too. Galt and his associates stood in the forest, still dripping from a day of great rain, as the sun set on a summer evening of 1827, and with the axe passed from hand to hand, they felled on a rising knoll a great maple tree to mark the site of a town. This done the axe was exchanged for a circulating flask of whisky, and a health was drunk to the prosperity of the future city—the present city—of Guelph. The company founded likewise Stratford and Galt, placed 4,500 settlers in the Huron district, and built up a settlement at Goderich that numbered four families in 1829 and 5,000 people ten years later. Its activity covered the period just proceeding responsible government and its legal shadow lingers still.

It is characteristic of the time that another company, the Columbian Agricultural Association, was founded in London alongside of the Canada Company with the patriotic object of settling Highlanders in Venezuela. Providence visited this enterprise as it deserved. Its destitute survivors were conveyed to Upper Canada. There was also the British American Land Company (1834), which was given an Imperial charter permitting it to buy 3,000,000 acres in British North America. In actual fact, it only took up land, with no great success, in the eastern townships of Quebec. The claim of the local legislature to jurisdiction frustrated its efforts.

.   .   .   .

These efforts, public, private and corporate were not without success. They indicate, as will be shown in a later chapter, exactly the line of policy to be followed now on a vast scale and with an industrial technique of which Galt never dreamed. There were great difficulties. At the best, population tended to drain away to the United States. It had the larger population, the long start and the easy accessibility of its roads, its new canals and its newer railroads. But till responsible government began in 1840, Canada held the balance almost even. British migration was divided. In the first quarter-century that elapsed after 1815 (the years 1815 to 1840) a total of 1,164,713 emigrants, or 44,796 each year, left the British Isles. The low tide of migration was represented by the 12,510 emigrants of 1816, the flood by the 103,140 of 1832. Nearly all of these went to North America. Migration to Australia was of no account till the political troubles in Canada and the notoriety of Wakefield's schemes of colonization gave it a great impetus. Only 29,982 people went to Australia as emigrants in the period 1815 to 1835, an annual average of 1,149. From 1835 to 1841 no less than 86,320 migrated to the Antipodes, a movement to be examined later in this chapter. For the period 1815 to 1841 emigration from the British Isles to places other than British North America, the United States, Australia and New Zealand only included 348 people each year, a total of 9,072, a factor entirely negligible.

To North America there went from 1815 to 1840 a total of 990,826 emigrants, and of these 532,419 to British North America and 458,407 to the United States.

But with the institution of responsible government, the situation entirely changed. In the next quarter of the century (1841–66), which happens to correspond with the life of the old (united) Province of Canada, the total emigrants to the United States numbered 2,639,863 and those to British North America only 677,036. This was precisely the period when began the great modern exodus out of Europe. Circumstances conspired to cause and to accelerate its volume. Steam transport on the ocean and the steam-boat and railway made movement easy and cheap as never before. At the same time Europe seemed unable to support its population. There were a million paupers in England in 1842. In Ireland the potato crop failed (1845–6–7), and famine walked like a spectre through the land. When crops failed, rent failed. Alien landlords cast out the evicted tenant to die, or to emigrate as best he could. One hundred and sixty thousand people were evicted in Ireland in the years 1847, 1848 and 1849 ; they died in hundreds by the roadside ; they died in hundreds in the sea-ports ; they died in hundreds in the ships. And those who did not die, gaunt, famished and stinking with the filth and squalor of the emigrant ship, reached, as a long-sought haven, the shores of the United States. The harvest, planted thus for Eng-land, is not all gathered even yet. During the grim years of the decade of the forties, a million people died in Ireland and a million and a half, mostly with hatred in their hearts, migrated to America.

Continental Europe, convulsed by the revolutions of 1848, sent forth a stream of political refugees to be the Pulitzers and the Carl Schurzes of America. The leaven of liberty that should have tempered German autocracy was cast into the melting-pot of the United States. Political migration soon turned into economic. In the twenty years before the Civil War, there came to the United States 1,380,000 Germans, a movement which only slackened when the vigorous economic policy of the German Empire showed its people how to live at home.

Public opinion on both sides of the ocean favoured migration. In the United States, at this time, fortunately for the new-comers, the whole trend of thought and national policy favoured increase of numbers. It was held to build up the country. The new-comers arrived in a state of poverty and destitution beyond belief. But they were welcome. As yet the doctrine of " bread and work for all " prevailed, the sound economic idea that new un-developed country must be all the better for having immigrants, had not yet been replaced by the one-eyed vision of the labour economist. There was no dream of a quota law. There was, as yet, no biological idea of a Nordic race too pure to mix : in those days a mixed race, if not compounded with black and yellow, was regarded with as much favour as a mixed drink. In England public opinion, which at times had revolted against loss of population, came round more and more strongly to the idea of emigration. The economists could find no other remedy. Even the noble John Stuart Mill, looking out on the " probable future of the labouring classes " in 1848, could see nothing better ahead of them than either to stay at home, work hard and have no children, or else to migrate out of England. The cosmopolitan idea, noble in conception, but false in fact, that all the world was one, made no distinction between migration to a British colony and migration to an American republic. So well had Malthus and Cobden done their work.

The emigration idea laid hold even of our literature. The Victorian novelists could find no better method of transformation of their characters, of their redemption from sin, rescue from evil, or escape from poverty, than to send them off to the Antipodes. There Mr. Micawber became a merry magnate, and there little Emily's tears are dried away in the shadow of the eucalyptus. Dickens sent so many of his characters to Australia that he ended by sending his son after them.

Meantime, there was added, just at the close of the period of which we speak, in favour of the United States, the powerful attraction of the Homestead Law (1862). This acted like a forced draught to a furnace already burning hard. The Act represented a policy of " free homes for all ", which had been an uppermost idea in America politics for a generation. The jealousy of the slave-holding South had kept it off the statute-books. With its passage, new-comers immediately after the Civil War flocked into the farm-land of what is now called the Middle West. The law, like the present Canadian statute, gave 160 acres (a quarter-section) to every citizen head of a family. Twenty-seven million acres were taken between 1867 and 1874. In the ten years after the Act, 2,065,000 immigrants came from Europe to the United States, of whom forty-five per cent were British and thirty-four per cent were German. In the one year 1873 there came 460,000 immigrants.

So passed the middle of the century, a period, in the reckoning of migration, all to the bad for England and all to the good for the United States.

The Homestead Law exactly met and matched the circumstances of the day in the United States. Its great success then and later has concealed from sight its utter inadequacy to meet the present situation of the Empire. It remains as a misleading guide to policy : a stumbling-block to the feet of progress.

. . . .

Meantime in another part of the British Empire at this same epoch there was initiated an entirely different plan of migration in which perhaps may be found the solution of the present imperial problem. This was the " systematic colonization " scheme of Edward Gibbon Wakefield. This scheme, after an initial period, of roseate hope, collapsed in apparent failure, and left nothing but debris to be rebuilt on a better plan. Apparently what went up as a rocket came down as a stick. But the seeming failure was only like that of Langley's flying machine which flew into the Potomac in 1896. The real success was there. If migration in the Empire is to be co-ordinated with land and capital it is from the fundamental ideas of Wakefield's system that we must start anew. The homestead system has nothing to say to the man living on the dole in Birmingham and unable to pay his way to Canada.

. . . .

Edward Gibbon Wakefield (1796–1862) was a young Englishman of decent family and education who went to Newgate prison, quite deservedly, for three years in 1837 for having kidnapped an heiress. Prison sharpened his wits, or at any rate his sympathies. These were the good old days of the transportation of criminals. Many of Wakefield's fellow-unfortunates were bound for the long voyage to Botany Bay ; others were to embark, just outside the prison, on a voyage longer still. Wakefield wrote, and his words came as one of those voices from prison which have reached humanity with such poignancy from Cervantes and Bunyan to Oscar Wilde and Julian Hawthorne. His *Punishment of Death* and its message to the world belongs elsewhere. But his *Letter from Sydney* (1829), developed later into his *Art of Colonization*, opened a new chapter in the history of European migration, and has stamped its effect on a large portion of the present empire.

. . . .

Wakefield's central idea, as propounded to the House of Commons by his friend Charles Buller in 1843, was " to make colonization an extension of civilized society instead of that mere emigration which aimed at little more than shovelling out paupers to where they might die, without shocking their betters with the sight or sound of their last agony ". Wakefield saw that for " systematic colonization " land, labour and capital are all needed. These must be co-ordinated and balanced. A connection must be made between " the boundless regions wanting people " and " the countless people wanting land ". This connection was to be made through capital, and the capital was to be obtained by the sale of the public land. The previous haphazard systems of colonial policy, so Wakefield argued, had led to an abundance of land, a lot of it, like the Clergy Reserves in Canada and the great blocks in the Swan River Settlement, unoccupied and unused, a mere encumbrance to real settlement. At the same time " the absolute want of hands at any rate of wages in a colony " precluded economic advance. Wakefield therefore proposed a sort of endless chain of prosperity. The Government would survey and sell the public land ; with the money received they would give free passage to emigrants from England. On arrival in the colony these immigrants would hire as labourers. In a year or two they would save enough money to buy land and hire others to work for them. The price they paid would bring out more labourers : hence still more land occupied ; more capital ; more immigrants—and so on till the

colonial wilderness should blossom like the gardens
of England.

Wakefield, very properly, kept away from details
too exact : at what price should the land be sold ?
At a " sufficient price ", according to place and
circumstance. What wages should be paid to the
new-comers ? Sufficient wages. " To name a price
for all the colonies ", said Wakefield, " would be as
absurd as to fix the size of a coat for mankind."

Wakefield's theories were received, so wrote Professor Merivale thirty years later, " by the multitude
with incredulity, by the learned with scorn ". Yet
they made headway. Opposed at first by the
Times, the *Edinburgh* and by the whole phalanx of
Conservative opinion, they presently won over the
Press and captured the Colonial Office. John Stuart
Mill, Colonel Torrens and other economists rallied
in support. A " Colonization Society " was founded
to exploit the plan, and in the decade following
(1830–40) the Wakefield scheme of colonization
was tried out in Australia and New Zealand—tried
out and, in appearance, failed. In reality the
circumstances of the experiment were such that
the system never had a chance. But unfortunately
for imperial development, the apparent failures in
Australia ruled the Wakefield plan out from further
practical application, and led to the adoption of the
inadequate homestead system as the method of
colonization throughout the Empire.

There was scarcely any emigration of free settlers
from England to Australia from the beginning of the
nineteenth century to the formation of the Colonization Society of 1830. Till 1828 there were less

than a thousand a year, and in some years only three or four hundred. But in the decade of the 'thirties, distress in England swelled the volume of prospective emigrants at the very time when hard times and political troubles in the Canadas were discouraging emigration in that direction. Emigration to British North America, which had reached 60,000 in 1832, sank to 15,000 in 1835 and to 4,000 in 1838. Attention naturally turned to Australia as a field for emigration, and in particular as the proper site for an experiment in systematic colonization. Unfortunately the Australian colonies already existing, in spite of the insignificant number of their population, were already badly damaged as a field for the new system. Lavish and unsystematic grants of lands had set up huge holdings. In the parent colony of New South Wales land had been recklessly granted. Until 1822 a tract of land could be obtained by merely " sitting down " on it. A simple promise to occupy the land, handed in to the surveying department in writing, set up a claim. One military officer received 15,000 acres because the Governor " was inclined to think he might settle there ". By the year 1825 when this loose system at last received a check, 340,000 acres had been granted on such vague promises of occupation. Things were no better in Van Dieman's Land (Tasmania) ; though the population was only 20,000 and the land occupied and cultivated only 56,000 acres, the grants of land had already alienated a million and a half acres. The newly founded Swan River Colony (Western Australia) (1828) was the worst of all. While the colony was less than a year old and had only 850 settlers, already 525,000 acres had been granted away. The huge grants of land were worse than useless for actual settlement, which was impeded by their existence. They served only as a basis for land speculation and as an incentive to further grants. Trading in land took the place of working the land.

．　．　．　．　．　．　．　．

The English disciples of the Wakefield idea decided therefore to avoid the existing settlements and to start a colony of their own. A South Australian Association was formed and secured (1834) an Act "to erect South Australia into a British Province, and to provide for the colonization and the government thereof". Commissioners were appointed who were to borrow £200,000 from private sources and on the credit of the revenues of the future colony, not guaranteed by the Imperial Government. Theoretically this fund was to pay the cost of sending out the emigrants, establishing a port of settlement and surveying and allotting the lands. Theoretically also the proceeds of the sales of land would reimburse the original loan, and the productive output of the colony would then produce a revenue for further operations. Iu practice all was confusion. There was delay in choosing the commissioners. When chosen they quarrelled, resigned and were replaced. Lack of confidence made it impossible to raise money to begin, until a London magnate, George Angas, formed a private company to put money into the venture to start it going. There were quarrels as to how to sell the land—fixed price, graded prices or auction sales. Wakefield himself dropped out in disgust. All this in England, but worse when the " colony " reached its destination. Fifteen shiploads of immigrants (nearly 1,000 people) were deposited at the site of the future settlement (Adelaide). But the land was not yet surveyed and not ready for selection ; so the immigrants sat about in idleness, made merry and quarrelled and speculated in land script for the unallotted land. This delayed all productive settlement. Public relief works had to be started to keep the emigrants at work for pay. The resources of the colony were eaten up in such fruitless operations without economic return. More and more settlers came in and less and less capital. By 1840 there were 14,600 settlers in the colony, of whom 8,400 were still sitting round in the capital. Finally an Imperial Act of 1842 wound up the colony, as far as its special features of colonization went. The Imperial Government made good a deficit of £215,000 involved in the failure of the project. But in reality the scheme had only failed as any other first attempt—a first steam engine, a first flying machine—is apt to fail. It was the details of the mechanism that were at fault, not the principle of the machine.

A similar experiment, but with a much larger measure of success, was presently tried out in New Zealand. It was characteristic of the lack of economic foresight of the *laissez-faire* period that the British Government tried hard for many years not to own or annex or colonize New Zealand. The beautiful " long white cloud " lay almost untenanted and quite unclaimed—a land of wonderful fertility and resources, equal in area to Great Britain, and occupied only by some 120,000 natives. The claim of the Maori was as great and as small as that of any other savages who occupy, to the extent of about one person to a square mile, territory which they can only utilize to a fraction of its worth and the resources of which they cannot even understand. But by an Act of Parliament of 1817 England had expressly denied all sovereignty over the islands. Even when a New Zealand Association was formed (1837) every possible objection and hindrance was raised and a bill to incorporate the association was rejected by Parliament. Meantime individual settlers had established themselves here and there, buying land in great blocks for hatchets, guns and beads. There came also traders and others of doubtful character. The missionaries of the Church of England and of the dissenting bodies were at work among the natives, and had in the course of their ministrations secured large tracts of land. They and their supporters at home were against all colonization, preferring the vision of the Christianized savage reclaimed from his own peculiar wickednesses, such as cannibalism, without adopting those of civilization. Already the new fascination of using gunpowder in fighting was decimating the Maori.

Against all these false values the colonization scheme had to make its way. Luckily the news that the French were about to establish a sovereignty caused the British Government to make a right-about-face in policy. A treaty made at Waitanga in 1840, and signed by 512 native chiefs, established the British claim. Meantime the New Zealand

Association, failing a special charter, had turned itself into a stock company, collected £100,000 and sent out (1839) ships with agents to purchase lands for its settlements. It won Gibbon Wakefield, who had first formed the New Zealand Association, and his brother Colonel Wakefield was in charge of the first expedition. The whole scheme of colonization thus set on foot was based on Wakefield's essential idea of free transit for emigrants, work by emigrants for wages, and the purchase of land by the company at first out of subscription funds and later out of receipts. But the general plan was much confused in the details of its operation, so that the scheme and its subdivisions were in the end neither altogether governmental nor philanthropic or commercial. Though it came to an end in 1852 with the Act organizing the government of New Zealand, it was certainly far from being a failure. The company in its first year (1839–40) brought out 1,350 immigrants. Labourers going out to work for wages were carried free. Four years later emigration to New Zealand amounted to nearly 9,000 a year. A branch of the parent company settled New Plymouth with 532 emigrants in one year. A more important offshoot was the Presbyterian settlement at Dunedin organized in 1845. Its originators bought 144,000 acres from the New Zealand Company and the settlers landed at Otago in 1848. By 1854 there was a population of 2,400, and a town of Dunedin so named, in fond memory of Edinburgh, with 700 people and the outline of a college. Most completely organized was the settlement at Canterbury (1850). This was to be a true Wakefield colony. Land was to be sold at a fixed price of £3 per acre; of the money received ten shillings was to go to the New Zealand Company as original purchaser of the land, ten shillings to make roads, etc.; £1 to the Church and education and finally £1—or one-third of the money paid—became a fund to bring out more emigrants. The Canterbury Association remained in operation as a colonizing scheme till 1853. In all, about 13,000 immigrants were assisted in coming to the colony; others came by themselves, so that by the year 1852, when the various colonization schemes terminated, there was a white population in New Zealand of 31,000. Great difficulties had been encountered. Of the vast purchases made for the New Zealand Company by Colonel Wakefield, amounting to 20,000,000 acres, a great part was declared irregular and void, and the claim cut to 320,000 acres. In many cases, as at Canterbury, the price put on the land was too high to effect a wide enough sale. At Dunedin the receipts were too low to pay for the necessary operation of settlement. In the final adjustment of debit and credit the Government of New Zealand wound up the land company by paying it £200,000 in settlement of its claim.

To many people, and as told in many of the books, the South Australian and New Zealand experiments appear as a mere curiosity of colonial history. They passed out of public attention and public policy. The American homestead system, and the enormous migration which seemed to crown it with success, obscured the real superiority of the Wakefield plan. The homestead system is for those who have, but the Wakefield system is for those who have not. For the American farmer of the year 1900 moving into Saskatchewan with a carload lot of machinery and furniture and a capital and credit of $1,000 per head for each of his family, the homestead system supplies exactly the magnet needed. The lure of the land, the magic of property are embodied in it. But for the workless man in the streets of London or Glasgow, what has the homestead system to say ? Nothing.

And to-day the whole problem of migration is the problem of the workless man. If we want to solve it we must turn back to the plans and schemes of John Galt and George Angas and Gibbon Wakefield.

.   .   .   .

By the time of the American Civil War and the Homestead Act (1862) and the great western movement which followed the war, the period of systematic colonization was at an end. Henceforth " assisted migration " was only on a minor scale, as a form of philanthropy, not as a national policy. It was in the period from 1860 to 1900 that Great Britain should have triumphed in a migration and settlement policy. The United States for four years was overwhelmed with the terrific struggle of the Civil War. If England had known enough to build a Pacific railway, to open up the West and British Columbia, to put settlers in to the full extent of the British surplus population and with full power of British capital and to reach across the ocean to the Orient, the economic consequences would have been colossal. But England knew nothing of the sort. The United States recovered rapidly from the war and took up with characteristic energy the western movement of settlement interrupted (though never quite terminated) by the conflict. The Central Union Pacific route opened transcontinental traffic in 1869. The Northern Pacific to Portland (Oregon), the Southern Pacific linking New Orleans to San Francisco, and the Sante Fé route from centre to south-west were completed within fifteen years more. What seemed a boundless area of new land was thus available. The opening of the great wheat plains of Minnesota and the Dakotas challenged the invention of the incomparable machinery that gave them their full meaning. Immigration poured over the west in a flood. Between the end of the Civil War and the close of the century (1865–1900), migration from Europe to the United States amounted in all to 12,635,000. There was an annual average of over 300,000. From the British Isles the whole total of migration during this period was 9,767,817, and of this total no less than 6,914,303 went to the United States, to Canada only 1,092,001.

Look at some of the notable years. The figures are almost pathetic. The year 1870—the year of the foundation of the province of Manitoba—saw 196,000 British people migrate to the United States and only 35,000 to British America. In 1881— with the Manitoba boom " booming "—307,000 British went to the United States, 34,000 to British America. In 1886, the year of the opening of the Canadian Pacific Railway from coast to coast, only 30,000 came to British America and 238,000 to the

United States. There is no break in the record till the century turned and passed. The economic reason for this is all too clear in retrospect. When Canada took over the North-west in 1869 it had not the power, the capital, the wealth to develop it. All Canadians read and admire the story of the opening of the great North-west, a wonderful story of courage and confidence—heroic, considering the limited numbers and the limited means of the people who achieved it. But in the cold light of economic analysis, how utterly inadequate were the means adopted as compared with the means that lay ready to hand. England, with the boundless capital of the 'seventies and 'eighties, could have sent in an army of contractors and workers, as they were sent over half the world, and built the railway with a northern section of it to Prince Rupert, and followed it with 200,000 settlers a year.

Let it be observed what happened when the inadequate Dominion of Canada tried to open the west. The first opening led to the Manitoba Land Boom—which was quite sound at the base—and the collapse of the boom—which was needless, and a stagnation of twenty years. The transfer of the North-west from the Hudson's Bay Company to Canada was followed by the creation of the province of Manitoba in 1870. It contained only 12,000 inhabitants, of whom 558 were Indians and 9,840 half-breeds. Access was difficult and little was known of the fertility of the country. For years neither knowledge nor capital was forthcoming. After the opening of the province the population only rose to 36,000 in 1876. But after that the establishment of rail connection with St. Paul and the definite prospect (1881) of a Canadian Pacific Railway started a movement of migration from the older provinces, and a sudden realization of the possibilities of the North-west that precipitated the Manitoba Boom of 1881–3. Settlers flocked in. There was apparently the sudden miracle of occupation for all, credit for all, fortune for all. Town lots were staked out for miles into the prairie. The population of Winnipeg rose to 10,000 in 1881 and nearly 20,000 two years later. Adjacent settlements of a few shacks and tepees turned into " cities ". Land at Portage la Prairie rose from two dollars and a half an acre to sixty dollars.

. . . .

The Manitoba Boom collapsed in 1883. The banks and others who had lent money called it in : credit came to an end, and the incipient settlement of the North-west collapsed like a balloon without gas. It was explained at the time, and ever since, that the movement had been too rapid and that a check was bound to come. This is economic nonsense. The movement was too slow. The rosiest estimates of the boom time fell far short of the reality. Winnipeg, with its present population of 300,000, is an actuality and could have been an actuality a quarter of a century sooner. 380,639 homestead settlers took up land in Western Canada between 1904 and 1914. They could just as well have gone in between 1884 and 1894, when only 35,979 homestead entries were made. The wheat crop of Canada reached a record of 450,000,000 bushels in 1928. The land was there to grow it in

1884. There are over 2,000,000 people living in the prairie provinces to-day : the means for their support were all there in 1884. All that was needed was to keep the land boom going with more and more capital. Nowadays it is related in derision that there were forty real estate offices in Portage la Prairie in 1882. So there should have been. They needed them, with half a continent to divide up. The fault is not that the real estate offices were opened, but that they ever had to be closed.

.   .   .   .

The opening years of this century till the War showed a better record. The volume of British emigration was greater than ever, a total of 6,303,050 people for the years 1900–13 inclusive, or an annual average of 484,850. But the situation was entirely changed in that a much greater part of it than ever before since the beginning of responsible government was a migration from the British Isles to the British Dominions. In these fourteen years 3,416,587 British immigrants went to the United States, 430,333 to Australia, 425,659 to South Africa, and to Canada a total of 1,625,054. If we add to this that immigrants were coming into the North-west of Canada from the United States at the rate of about 100,000 a year we can see that the balance had turned. The free land in the United States really suitable for homestead farming was by this time practically used up. Much of the land first settled in the American West had deteriorated from over use and under fertilization. The American farmers moved, bag and baggage, into Canada. In the year 1897 only 730 persons had entered the

North-west as settlers from the United States; in
1900 there were 15,000; in 1911 the entry reached
100,000 and in 1913 the record mark of 139,000
immigrants. What happened then showed the
homestead system at its best, the conditions being
the only ones under which in modern surroundings
it is of value. The Americans who joined in the
" invasion " of the West were people of substance.
They paid their own transport and brought their
own goods. The Canadian Government estimated
that with each man, woman and child there came
into the West a thousand dollars' worth of money
and goods. The effect brought about thus under
conditions of the purely private initiative of individual people is exactly what could be done under a
colonization scheme of migration to-day. It represented the union of immigrants and capital with the
resources of fertile territory, the co-ordination of
the factors of land, labour and capital—the trinity
in whose power early economists saw the very source
and origin of wealth.

.   .   .   .

The American invasion slackened and ended.
Then the War came, and at its close the world had
changed. All the world henceforth thought in terms
of debts and deficits and unemployment. The
search for work that followed demobilization and
the crash of war prices in 1920 made it seem as if
every working man was the rival and enemy of
every other: as if " work " was a form of property
or asset divided up among claimants and com-
petitors. Thus the whole aspect of migration was
soon discoloured with the jaundice of false economic

teaching as to the relation of labour to wealth. The United States, to keep its "labour market" to itself, adopted under its quota laws a policy of partial exclusion. In all the Dominions the labour parties are prejudiced against immigrations. Unable to look any further than to the immediate distress of present unemployment, they do not see that perhaps the remedy for unemployment is to bring in more labourers—provided the capital comes with them.

As a result of this, all the various attempts at assisted immigration in the Empire since the War have been half-hearted, only partially successful, and on too small a scale to count for anything. Much was expected after the War. An Overseas Settlement Committee was instituted (1917) and free ocean passages secured for ex-service men and their families. Under this plan in four years of operation 86,000 persons migrated out of Great Britain— 28,000 to Canada, 34,000 to Australia, 12,000 to New Zealand and about 6,000 to South Africa. But the scheme was obviously of no permanent value unless conjoined with some positive action for placing the emigrants and supplying capital to work with them. A Colonial Office conference in London in 1921 recommended that the Governments of Great Britain and the Dominions should co-operate in a policy of assisted settlement. The conference of prime ministers accepted and endorsed the suggestion. So did everybody. The difficulty was to give it effect. The division of jurisdiction brought about by the disintegration of the Empire left no one with complete control. As a result the Empire Settlement Act of 1922, though admirable in principle, is almost abortive in operation. By this Act the British Government authorizes the Secretary of State to join in any plan of assisted migration with any Dominion Government or with public or private authorities in Great Britain or the Dominions to the extent of bearing half the cost of the enterprise. The money expended from the British exchequer must not be more than £3,000,000 in any one year. The Act is to last till 1937.

In the eight years that have followed the adoption of the Act a number of schemes have been entered into as between the British Government and those of the Commonwealth of Australia—the states of Western Australia, Victoria, and New South Wales, the Dominion of Canada and certain organizations in South Africa. The agreements provided for assisted ocean passages which, in the case of Canada, were confined to farm labourers and domestic servants : a stipulation which reminds us that " hired men " and " hired help " are of the class of unorganized labour and cannot protest. Skilled labour in Canada holds as jealously as elsewhere to the idea that a new-comer steals the job of the man on the spot. Western Australia undertook to settle 75,000 people in three years and to raise and spend £6,000,000, of which the Imperial Government was to pay one-third of the interest for five years. Victoria was to raise £3,000,000 and at once to settle 2,000 persons as owners and occupiers of farms. The Canadian Government agreed to provide improved farms for 3,000 families. An agreement on a much greater scale was arranged in 1925 as between

Australia and Great Britain. This was to settle 450,000 immigrants in the Commonwealth in ten years. For these Australia was to raise in total loans, including those already guaranteed for the states, the sum of £34,000,000 and the Imperial Government to contribute £130,000 for each £750,000 raised in the Commonwealth. In South Africa a Settlers Association was organized to co-operate with the British Government in assisted passages, loans for settlers and the creation of training farms. Minor arrangements were made by the Imperial Settlement Act with the Canadian Pacific Railway, with the Scottish Immigrant Aid Society and other bodies.

.   .   .   .

It would be unfair to belittle the importance of the Empire Settlement Act. The underlying principle of co-operation and union of resources rests on the true basis of Imperial integration. But the results thus far fall far short of anticipations, and as compared with the vast problem of Empire migration, with the vast scale of our national resources and the present appalling devastation of unemployment—compared, in other words, with the work to be done—the results are almost insignificant. In five years of operation the Victorian scheme only established 401 families and the New South Wales plan 327. The Western Australian group settlement came to an end. It was found that the cost of establishing a farm in Australia is £1,500 and that this cost was entirely prohibitive. The settler could stay in London and live on the interest of this without going to Australia at all.

New Brunswick had placed about 200 families by the end of 1929. The Canadian Government supplied 2,500 specially trained British hired men to western farmers. The 1928 experiment of sending 8,000 British workers, mostly from the coal mines, to help with the harvest work in the Canadian North-west was about as successful as would be the sending of 8,000 Canadian farmers to help with the mines.

In the five years 1923-7 the total British emigration numbered 872,000, of whom 649,000 went to the Overseas Empire and 223,000 to foreign countries. The closing of the United States to all except the quota rendered this choice of destination not entirely free : 245,000 emigrants received assisted passages. But in spite of all the facilities afforded by the Act, the volume of migration is less than it was before the War, without State subsidies, when in 1913 to Canada alone there went 143,000 British emigrants. The year 1928 showed a still further decline to 136,000 emigrants as compared with 153,000 in 1927. Of these emigrants those to British North America numbered 54,000, to Australia 28,000, to New Zealand 5,000 and to South Africa 7,000. Statistics available for the year 1929 show 53,264 emigrants as the net emigration from the United Kingdom to British North America, with only 8,861 to Australia.

. . . .

Take it all in all it is quite plain that something far more comprehensive is needed than the present colonization system. The present system makes heavy demands of the taxpayer but fails to supply adequate capital. What is wanted is a proposal into which there will enter along with the taxpayer and the emigrant a third person, forgotten since the days of John Galt and Gibbon Wakefield—the investor. But before his part in the transaction can be considered we must pass in review the growth and the export of British capital.

CHAPTER V

THE EXPORT AND INVESTMENT OF BRITISH CAPITAL

IT is commonly estimated that at the time of the outbreak of the Great War the amount of British capital invested outside of the British Isles amounted to about four thousand million pounds—or what is called, with the word billion used in our transatlantic signification, twenty billion dollars. This outflow represented, almost entirely, money used by private persons and by private companies in Great Britain to buy shares and securities in foreign and colonial companies, subscriptions to government loans and public debts and all advances of money of that sort. It does not include, since no statistics could be available, money and goods carried out of the country by immigrants in various forms. If it did, the sum total would be considerably greater.

This outward flow of money and of documents representing money is, however, only an external appearance. The reality consists in the outward flow of actual goods and services of which the money is the symbol, the evidence and the mechanism.

The great migration of capital and capital goods had its basis in the eighteenth century, which created an actual surplus of goods ready to export. These goods were not merely things to consume, but goods, the consumption and use of which would create wealth greater still. England's productive surplus was applied to develop the opportunities of less favoured or of newer countries.

The outflow of capital began at once after the Napoleonic War. In its relation to Imperial development, its history during the hundred years from the end of one great war to the beginning of the next may be divided into three periods, each corresponding, roughly, to the third of a century. During the first of these, which covers the great peace that lasted from 1815 till the Crimean War of 1854, the period of the rising free trade and Cobdenism, hardly any of the export of capital went to the British Empire. If we follow, where all exactness is lost in conjecture, so excellent a guide as Mr. L. H. Jenks, British external investment during this period amounted to a total of from one hundred and ninety-five to two hundred and thirty million pounds. Of this the United States received about one-quarter, investment in Government securities in Europe took from eighty to one hundred million pounds, the Latin America republics £35,000,000. The building of colonial railways with British funds had not begun till just at the end of this epoch, and the sums invested in Australian or Canadian land companies as mentioned above were too small to matter.

A second division may be found in the declining period of *laissez-faire* and Cobdenism from the time of the Crimean War until the beginning of the New

Imperialism, which occasioned the renewed expansion of Europe in search of materials and markets, which led to the partition of Africa and (where possible) of Asia, and opened the epoch of high tariffs and economic world rivalry that ended with the outbreak of the Great War. The year 1880 may be taken as a dividing line. For the total investment of British capital at or about 1880 there are various estimates which place it at something like £1,200,000,000. But the division is now different. No less than £160,000,000 is represented by investment in Indian railways and Indian public debt. The public loans raised by the colonies (a chief item being the Australian loans for railways) were taken up in England to the extent of £50,000,000. Hence the British Empire had at this time the benefit of £210,000,000, or rather more than one-sixth of the British export of capital. The United States had received, as subscriptions to public debts, nearly as much. Investments in railways—including both the United States and South America—included £240,000,000, and the amount of money lent by British people in taking up various foreign government loans amounted to £500,000,000.

The next period (1880–1914) shows a different movement of the outgoing current of British capital, which is henceforth directed in an increasing degree towards the Dominions and possessions of the British Crown. The total, according to Sir George Paish's estimate, had reached at the end of 1913 the sum of £4,000,000,000, of which £3,700,000,000 was invested in securities publicly offered and subscribed and hence easily traceable as to destinations. The sum of £1,780,000,000 was invested in the Empire (outside of Great Britain) ; £754,000,000 in the United States ; £764,000,000 in Latin America and only £200,000,000 in European countries. It appears at a glance that the direction and location of British funds had entirely altered as between the opening and the close of the century in question. Colonial investment, from being negligible, has risen to be nearly half of the total. Investment in European countries, which formerly represented one-half, had sunk to one-twentieth. Investment, in one form or other, in the United States stands at more than one-sixth of the total.

Greater still is the change, if we consider the period following the Great War. The United States has now become the great creditor nation, not only in respect to the amount of money owed to the United States Government by European Governments as war loans and as reparations, but also in respect to capital subscribed by individuals in the United States to take up foreign securities and loans. This investment was estimated in 1926 at $11,125,000,000 : $3,010,000,000 lent in Europe ; $4,500,000,000 in Latin America ; $2,801,000,000 in Canada and Newfoundland, and $904,000,000 scattered broadcast. Foreign loans raised in the United States in 1927 reached a total of $2,382,000,000, of which $300,000,000 went to Canada.

But England is still an investing nation. According to the *Liberal Industrial Report* of 1928, Great Britain, though hard pressed in a dozen ways, is still a long way from being bankrupt. There is still a productive surplus, or "national saving" represented by the reserves and undivided profits of companies and the savings out of income by individuals, of about £500,000,000 a year. Of this the greater part goes back in one way or another into home industry ; but about £100,000,000 is available for investment abroad. The amount of capital issues raised in London for investment in British possessions and in foreign countries represented as between 1920 and 1927 a total of £871,964,000, or an annual average of £109,000,000. Of this sum £576,048,000 was invested inside the Empire and £295,916,000 outside of it. The contrast speaks for itself.

.   .   .   .

But what has gone above is only a statistical and illustrative introduction to a very difficult subject —the export of capital and its economic consequences, immediate and ultimate. British public finance and legislative policy has been governed for a hundred years with the idea that money is money, and capital is capital, and that interest is interest ; that if you lend £100 in Chile and get back £6 interest that is just as good as if you lent £100 in Lancashire or in Canada and got back £6 interest : because (so it is argued) even if you do send out British goods to Chile or give Chile the benefit of British services, you get back Chilean goods in return. The productive return to England—at first sight—is therefore just the same whether it comes from Lancashire or Canada or Chile. In other words, it is argued, the thing speaks for itself : money talks.

All of which is error : money doesn't talk. It

is the most deceptive thing in the world. All our economic thinking is confused by it. The only things that talk are facts. If you lend five dollars to Chile what you get back is not the whole return from it—only part : unless the Chilean to whom you lent it is a most inefficient person. You yourself may do as well in lending to a Chilean as to a man in Lancashire. But your country doesn't—not by half. But for this it is best to turn back to the beginning and to review the origin and export of capital from the British Isles.

. . . .

The migration of capital, as just said, is a subject worthy of much attention, which as yet has received relatively little. Economic thought has been mainly occupied with the analysis of industrial society and with the problem of industrial justice. It has been largely taken for granted during the last hundred years that capital would of itself go where it was most wanted and best employed. The orthodox political economy included an automatic theory of money whereby money, based on the free coinage of gold, regulated itself and needed only to be let alone. The same automatic theory was extended to the idea of the movement of capital. As a consequence the economic development of the world in the nineteenth century followed largely along the path marked out by the self-interest of the investor, as the investor understood it.

It is only when we look back over the history of the matter that we realize that the result was very far from favourable to the economic development of the British Overseas Empire. The principal result of the export of British capital for the first two-thirds of the century of its investment was to finance the European States, to keep the Latin American republics right side up, to build railways in France, Latin America and India, and, above all, to develop the productive resources of the United States. Only a very minor part of the first thousand million pounds invested abroad went to develop what we now call the Dominions of the Empire. Whether this could have been otherwise at that time is a question not easy to answer. Whether capital could have been controlled in its outflow with a view to public as well as private benefit is a debatable matter. But there is no doubt that the situation is different now. Capital to-day can respond to stimulus, direction and control as easily as any other factor of our regulated collective life.

For most people " capital " and " investment " are vague terms, entirely confused with money and documents, bank cheques and other things with which they have in themselves nothing to do. But by capital we mean in political economy—not in the money market—all the whole apparatus of things already made which are useful in making other things. Machines are capital—factories, railway equipment, telegraphs, business premises. In fact we have only to open our eyes and look about us and what we mostly see is capital. In a modern industrial city there is more capital in sight than scenery.

Capital began in the twilight of early civilization and grew from little to great, from primitive to mediæval, and from mediæval to modern. It assumed overwhelming importance in the machine age that began about a century and a half ago.

What we really mean, then, by the export of capital and the investment of capital abroad is the actual moving of physical things into a foreign country to aid in carrying on production. When England sent shiploads of railway equipment to Argentina that represented the export of capital in the plain simple sense.

But the movement and use of capital in the modern world could not get far unless there came into being some easy way of distinguishing its ownership, of transferring its ownership and of combining its ownership so that a little capital from a lot of people would combine to make a lot of capital. Equally necessary, also, was it to work out some expeditious methods of sale and delivery of the ownership of capital, to break it up into suitable units and parts, so that a person who had not the means to own and operate a steam ship or a gold mine could at least own and operate the thousandth or even the millionth part of it. To effect this there grew up in connection with capital a whole apparatus of exchange and transfer and certification and division of ownership. Money came first : metal coins and then, to make these go further, pieces of paper claiming to represent them. Later on, by the close of the eighteenth century, there was developed a whole elaborate process of banking and payment without using money at all, or only as payment for small change.

The English were not the first to establish banking : they were indeed among the last. But with the great growth of English trade and colonial interest in the eighteenth century, London became the place where the theory, use and practice of investment capital worked itself into completion. The Bank of England was established in 1694. With it came the funded public debt which reached £130,000,000 before the American Revolution. The debt at its origin seemed to the public about as disagreeable a thing as debts usually are. But oddly enough it turned into something else—a sort of fund which could be bought and sold, a repository of investment, a comfort of old age, an indispensable part of a monetary national economy. Moreover, it helped to create a type of a new thing, or a new type of an old thing, a corporate fund of investment money. It is true that the stock funds of the East India Company of 1600 and the Hudson's Bay Company of 1670 are older than the national debt, but it was not till the eighteenth century and even the nineteenth that the real impetus was given to corporate investment. One factor which aided in this was the increasing improvements in the mechanism of exchange. The use of cheques grew up in the eighteenth century, first in the form of bank-notes, half printed and half written, to suit any sum and occasion (1729) and presently (1793) in the form in which we know them now. The convenient meeting of bank clerks at the London coffee houses to " swap " balances and deliver orders turned, after about 1750, into a Clearing House. In a similar way the meetings for buying and selling funds and securities at Jonathan's Coffee

House that began in 1773 turned into the Stock Exchange. Likewise a certain coffee house set up by a Mr. Edward Lloyd in the reign of William III became a gathering-place for merchants interested in insuring ships, and became first an association and then the great marine corporation of Lloyds. This whole process was exactly what everybody now (outside of Tennessee) loves to call an "evolution", in the course of which there grew up the London money market as the centre of the world's finance.

The most powerful engine of all for industrial finance was the latest to develop to its real strength —the stock company or incorporated company—and later still its giant children, the trust and the merger. In the eighteenth century English law and English opinion looked on stock companies (apart from trading companies operating, like the East India, on a special charter) with a doubtful eye. The Bubble Act of 1720 had rendered them either illegal or of doubtful legality. Till an Act of Parliament after the Napoleonic War set them free their status was not clear, and they shared with the partnership the overwhelming liability of everybody for everybody else's debt. Nor was their economic advantage fully understood. Adam Smith, at one of many tunes when he nodded over his writing, saw little future for industrial companies. But they had to come. Industry was too big for even the largest purse. The coming of the railroad and the transatlantic ship cleared a huge field for corporate enterprise.

The adoption of limited liability (1858) made it possible for millions of shareholders to enter the

field. But long before this the London money
market and the London financial houses were well
started on their way. What they seemed to do was
to make loans out of funds gathered in London.
What they really did was to help spread all over the
world British goods from British ships. The produce
of the world came back as interest, or more typically,
stayed where it was as a new investment.

.   .   .   .

This process had already begun in the eighteenth
century before the outbreak of the Great War with
France. But investment took as its earliest form
the buying and selling of shares in the funds, and
in the canal and turnpike companies which had
acquired a legalized existence. After the Great War,
however, British foreign investment began in real
earnest. The first conspicuous example was the
raising of a loan to enable France to pay the war
indemnity of 700,000,000 francs exacted by the Allies
after Waterloo, and the annual 150,000,000 francs
required annually to support the army of occupation.
This loan, raised in London by the great firm of
Baring Bros., originally a concern trading in wool,
was a conspicuous success. But there were dis-
sentient voices. Even in those times, a century
before the days of General Dawes and Mr. Owen
Young, it seemed a little odd to simple minds that
we should first exact an indemnity and then give the
ex-enemy the money to pay it with. More perplexing still to some people was the economic
bearing of it. Correspondents to the Press urged
that this seemed like using English capital to build
up France. " The profitable employment of our

own, and not foreign people," wrote one of these, " constitutes the wealth and prosperity of the British Empire." But such voices went unheeded in the tumult of the triumphant doctrine of industrial liberty which declared that the use by each individual of his own capital in his own interest led, as by the guidance of an invisible hand, to the wealth of nations. The French loan was followed by loans to Spain, and with the true impartiality of the capitalist, to the revolutionary governments in the revolted colonies of Spain. Chile, Peru, Buenos Ayres, Colombia, Guatemala and Mexico all sought the London market. Much of the money for the loans was spent in England on ships and stores. There was a profit on the transaction " coming and going ". There were equally profitable loans to liberate Greece, most of which money never got to Greece at all, being taken out as advance interest, commissions and payment for ships that never sailed and supplies that never materialized. There is an obvious contrast between the ultimate gain, whatever it was, from this revolutionary finance, as compared with the total possible gain from productive investment in home industry and colonial development.

More productive, though again of doubtful aspect, were the continuous loans and investments in the United States and France in the period which followed (1830–54). British capital went out in a flood to build the canals and railroads of the American Republic and to establish the rapid growth of banks which financed the industrial expansion of that rising country. English money built the

Erie Canal. Within six years of the coming of the railroad (1833) $90,000,000 went into railways and canals in the northern States, and the greater part of this was raised in England. At the same time a brisk trade developed, in which English exports of tools, hardware, dry goods and railway equipment created an enormous balance over American cotton and produce shipped in return. This balance, and more than the balance, was reinvested in America, and represented by British holdings of State debts and of securities of railroads, banks and other companies. Seen in an instantaneous flashlight this looks like a picture of real prosperity and trade for both countries, a true example of Cobdenite economics. But the great gain was to America. It was in America that the physical effects were manifested, in the clearing of forests, the making of farms, the building of towns, the construction of roads—all that great energy and activity which converted the woodland and prairie of the Ohio Valley into the colossal industrialism of to-day.

And in return England had—what? Ownership. Ownership of shares and scrip and claim for interest that for the most part never came back as consumption goods but remained as further ownership. But what is ownership? Only a breath, a document. It can pass. It can cross the ocean, owner and ownership migrating together, to follow the goods that it has sent ahead, as when 15,000,000 of British people migrated to the United States. If a nation first sends out its capital, its machinery and goods and money to develop a new country, and then follows this up with a migration of its people, the final balance of advantage is not hard to strike. The " ownership ", being a thing of pen and ink, of accounts and documents and not of physical goods, may vanish, or at least lessen, more mysteriously still. When the American railroads collapsed into the hands of receivers in the middle 'seventies, a great mass of British ownership vanished into nothing. Yet the railways were still there. British holders lost enormous sums in selling their American securities during the Civil War and when the silver-money panic of the early 'nineties threw blocks of securities on the New York market. Yet the physical face of America was unchanged.

The first collapse came when the industrial and financial crisis of 1837 halted all American enterprise. A lot of British ownership vanished in repudiated State debts and defaulted securities. But there was still plenty for British capital to do. The coming of the railway turned England itself into a new country, with ability to absorb endless capital in creating a railway network. In the first ten years of railway building in England (1830–44) about 2,000 miles of railway had been built with an investment of £55,000,000. Then in the middle 'forties the " railway mania " broke over England. By 1849 there were 6,000 miles in operation and a capital invested of over £900,000,000. The economic consequences extended far beyond England. The English iron and steel industry was the first to learn how to make railway equipment. The business of organized railway contracting, involving knowledge and experience in a dozen directions, grew up as a British enterprise. The English became the railway builders for the world. To build the French railways, iron and materials, masters and men—the "navvies" of the trade—crossed the channel in a body. Between 1840 and 1870 British capital was applied under British direction to build railways in France, in Spain, Norway, Denmark, Italy, India, Brazil, Australia and the Argentine. Meantime the recovery of the United States from the catastrophes of 1837 led also to an era of railway building to construct the "trunk lines" from the lakes to the sea and to the Gulf of Mexico. Great quantities of English capital were invested in what became presently the New York Central system, the Illinois Central and the Baltimore and Ohio. A great part of this capital passed out of British ownership at an enormous loss when the turmoil of the Civil War led to the liquidation of almost all American investments.

To the Province of Canada before Confederation there went an investment of well over a hundred million dollars, represented by British subscriptions in the provincial loans and the ill-starred British flotation of the Grand Trunk Railway.

. . . .

This same process of external investment went forward continuously till the close of the nineteenth century, assuming now this form and now that, now going in one direction and now another, according to the hour and circumstance. Increasing sums went to India after the Mutiny and the establishment of direct government. The railway systems of the Australian colonies were built with British money. And above all, the British public subscribed in the later part of the nineteenth century to the loans of the European Governments. In the 'sixties and the 'seventies there were great flotations in London of the borrowings of foreign governments, to make wars in Europe, revolutions in America and industrial development everywhere. In twenty years 1860–1879 the loans of this sort amounted to £320,000,000. Up to this time, as Mr. Jenks points out, the loans were based purely on " business principles " without the "imperial" motive which appeared more strongly in the closing part of the century. The outflow of capital from Great Britain, including the reinvestment of interest from 1870 till the year 1912, as computed by Mr. C. K. Hobson in his admirable thesis on the *Export of Capital*, represents, with variations and zigzags, an increasing volume that reaches its largest size with the £226,000,000 of 1912. The currents slacken and at times even turn backward. American railroad failures and depression in the middle 'seventies bring it to a full stop. A foreign investment in 1890 of £82,000,000, representing in part the rush to invest in South African mines, is contrasted with the £13,000,000 of 1901 and the £11,000,000 of 1902 which reflect the effect of the South African war.

. . . .

Behind all these figures and statistics stands the economic question as to the bearing, present and ultimate, of British foreign investment on the welfare of the British people. Decade after decade the process went almost unchallenged. The economic thought of the Victorian Age took for granted that enlightened self-interest of the individual must be the best national guide. But later experience reveals more and more the limitations of the dogma. The complete individualism that was the goal of industrial and commercial policy three generations ago has passed away. Most of us, nearly all of us, would retain individualism as the basis of the State —with individual property and contract, individual inheritance, and individual gains and rewards apportioned to the productive contribution of the individual. But to attain this we interfere with and intrude upon freedom at every point. We regulate hours of work and even wages of work. We circumscribe inheritance and redefine our notions of property. We seek to attain true freedom by replacing the mere appearance of it with the reality. Is it possible that the disposition of capital should come, and should have come, under this same sort of limitation by a national control of individual free will ? Or if not by national control and coercion at least by national inducement, by making it more profitable for the individual to invest capital to the national advantage and less profitable to him to send it abroad ?

Is it not at least conceivable that the disposition of British capital for a century past has been in great measure a vast error ? What was really happening when British money was building railways in the United States and tramways in Argentine ? Is it possible that what England was really doing was building up a great civilization of cities, factories and farms in foreign countries and leaving its own inheritance unused ? Worse than that, was it perhaps building up at its own expense the very

145   L

instruments that tend now to destroy its economic life ? If so—and if England now is feeling the cruel pinch of unemployment, the heavy burden of taxes, the drag of worn-out industries whose wheezing and antiquated plants contrast ill with the glittering iron and polished steel of the " rationalized " industries of America and Germany—if this is so, may not the foundation of it lie, in part, in misleading use of British capital in the past ?

But even if it is so, it is not too late. The present era, the post-war era, is witnessing new phases of the transit of capital. There is now a huge ebb tide of capital ready to come back from the United States, and willing to flow, already flowing, into the Empire, in the form of investment in the Dominion of Canada. Round this fact should centre much of our present Imperial policy. It is my opinion that it is our proper plan to reverse the rôles of America and Britain. We should now use American money and American capital goods to build up our country just as British money built up America. But this controversial topic I propose to deal with in a later chapter in the second part of this book.

PART II
FROM NOW ON

CHAPTER I

A PROPOSAL FOR AN INTEGRATED TARIFF SYSTEM WITHIN THE EMPIRE

THE first part of this book was devoted to the discussion of the economic situation which has resulted from the history of the British Empire. It was meant to show that the Empire has been gradually disintegrated. The process which brought political freedom and autonomy brought also economic weakness. Capital and labour, land and resources have been broken apart.

In this second half of the book I propose to discuss the means that may be adopted for the economic integration of the Empire. These concern the union of resources, the union of credit and capital, and the united direction of migration. There is also concerned the readjustment of the fiscal and tariff systems of the Empire. In a sense, the regulation of the tariff is the least fundamental of the points to be considered. Tariff systems do not of themselves create national wealth. That depends upon national resources, national capital and labour. The tariff is a consequence, not a cause : and tariff policy in the Empire as elsewhere is secondary to the fundamental production of wealth. But the tariff has the peculiar advantage of offering an immediate means of approach. It represents something in which action can be taken immediately and effectively. This action can then lead on to greater changes. I therefore put the question of the tariff first. No subject is so difficult for British readers to approach. No subject is so beset with preconcerted ideas and prejudices. To discuss the tariff with a British public is like proposing to discuss red rags with a bull. There are many people in England to whom what is called free trade rests on hallowed ground. It stands, to them, for a great national triumph achieved after long suffering, obtained by enthusiasm and self-sacrifice and never to be thrown away. It has somehow got mixed up with liberty, with British freedom, with the tears of the factory children, with the triumphs of Victorian England, and with many things with which it has not the least connection. To such people protection is a cheat, and a protected manufacturer a licensed robber.

Equally prejudiced in many cases is the attitude of the protectionist. There are people who get the idea that because a tariff duty may sometimes be a good thing, it is therefore *always* a good thing ; that if a little of it is good, then a lot of it is better still ; that to buy anything from a foreigner is wicked ; that to let a dollar go out of the country is to lose it for ever. Such persons see in protection an economic miracle. It makes work, raises wages and prevents unemployment ; whenever it seems to fail it is only because there is not enough of it. To such minds an ideal national system of industry would be framed behind a Chinese wall of absolute exclusion.

. . . .

But an introduction to a subject difficult at home may be found by first talking about our neighbours. In this case we may find an inoffensive opening to a tariff discussion by consideration of our relations with the United States.

The outstanding fact in the present organization of the world is the political and economic dominance of the United States. There it stands like a huge colossus, its feet spread on its North American continent. It has in front of it its Statue of Liberty, warning off all free entry of foreigners ; and behind it and beside it its Congress, tightening up the quota law ; its tariff committee shutting out everything ; its vast standardized industries selling to everybody and buying from nobody ; its marines, waiting what to seize next ; its bankers collecting debts still due on the conquest of Europe ; and everywhere the raucous voice of its " talking movie " and the hum of its incomparable machinery. To represent it abroad is the American tourist, for whose advent and for whose dollars the humble sirens of Europe —of all the world—sit anxious and expectant. America dominates the world. No one can talk back to the United States. They shut out the English, and the English dare not retaliate. They seal up every ship in their harbours, and no one dare object to it. Imagine if Siam had instituted such a law ! The proud might of the British navy would have seen to that in a minute. But in the case of the United States there is not any proud might of anybody, British, French, or anything. America is too powerful : Europe too divided.

A lot of this eminence has come to the United

States most deservedly. No nation ever worked so hard. No nation ever developed so clever a craft of invention. No nation ever gave to its people such an apparatus of education at so low a cost, such vast opportunities at home, so little social prejudice to combat, and, apart from the negroes who don't count, never counted and never will, so little of cast and inherited rights to obstruct the path of individual ambition. Nor did a country ever repeat such a harvest of public benefit and general welfare from the inspired gifts and endowments of its millionaires.

Under such circumstances the United States was bound to be a great country. It is a great country. But it is not nearly so great a country as it thinks it is, nor as the outside world fancies it. It would be vain imagining to say that this colossus has feet of clay and that it could be pushed over and smashed at any time. But it could at least be given, in all friendliness, a jolt that would shake it to its base. The thing called economic dominance can be terminated at any time.

The United States, unconsciously to itself, has become economically dependent upon the outside world. It cannot live without it. The vast army of its middle-west farmers would choke to death if they tried to eat their own food product ; the motor-car industry must keep up its world sales or go broke ; the hoarse voice of the talking movie must either be heard by the Polynesian savages or it must sink to a whisper at home. In other words, America cannot maintain the present structure and size of its great industry without the export trade ; and its export trade, at present, is on a peculiarly fragile basis. It gets everything and gives nothing. For its access to the markets of the British Empire, its greatest market, without which its trade must perish, it concedes nothing at all.

When the Americans discuss a new tariff proposal, as in the debates on the Fordney-McCumber tariff, and the Harley-Smoot bill of 1930, the last thing they think of is how the foreigner will feel about it, or what the foreigner will do about it. Up till now there has been nothing that the foreigner could, or would, do about it, and his feelings were three thousand miles away and didn't matter. All this was fair enough—in the world in which we live. So it came about that the Americans from first to last made their tariff to suit themselves. The few little items of reciprocity that ever appeared in it, such as the bygone compact with Canada and the present compact with Cuba, never marred the symmetry of its outline. The first tariff, that of 1789, in response to the ideas of Alexander Hamilton, put on mildly protection duties, about eight and a half per cent, to keep out, or check, the import of British manufactures. After the war of 1812 protection for New England was a settled policy. The South still wanted easy imports. Till the Civil War the question was an open one, with a tariff higher or lower according to party dominance. But there was no retaliation to fear : England had wedded itself to free trade and the union seemed permanent. In any case, the United States at this time could always " live on its own " if it wanted to ; in fact, it largely did so. It had no need of the foreigner.

Its vast territory extended through 3,000 miles over which actual settlement moved forward with every decade.

With the Civil War came a real tariff, raised to the brim, with either revenue or protection for everything. The little episode of reciprocity with Canada (1855–66) was washed out. It was never renewed. Canadian supplications and pilgrimages to Washington (1864–99) met a deaf ear. Canada, as the prospect of annexation passed away, was put into the foreign class. The Civil War tariff was never removed. Changes in it made it more strictly protective and distinguished between the material of manufacture and finished goods ; but that was all. The system was, and is, there to stay. It long outgrew its original arguments. Its infant industries grew into giants. The little baby suit of the United States steel industry was stretched to bursting, but was never taken off. The war exigencies altered to the gorged opulence of peace. But the war tariff stayed. With the national republican platform of 1888, protection in the United States threw off all shame and announced itself as a national, permanent policy. The McKinley tariff of 1890 carried it into effect with protection for everything and everybody. For the farmer the tariff on barley (these were the days of Milwaukee beer) was raised from ten to thirty cents a bushel ; on wheat from twenty to twenty-five ; on potatoes from fifteen to twenty-five, and so on all along the line. The imposition of a tariff on eggs showed that the consumer was dead.

Labour, now organized and powerful, was similarly protected. The Alien Labour Contract Laws of 1885 and 1889 were designed to stop the flooding of the labour market with foreign importations.

In all of this there was nothing that went beyond the ordinary, recognized right of a nation to run its own business. But it must, of course, carry with it the right of other nations to act similarly. The answer to the quota law ought to be to shut Americans out of Paris and to forbid them to fish in the hotels of Quebec. But alas ! neither the French nor the Canadians nor the British are in a position to think of this.

On this exclusive system—which had the good luck not to meet enough retaliation to hurt it— the United States flourished mightily. It secured its own enormous and growing market. The steel rails that used to be rolled at Birmingham were made at Pittsburg. Its enormous export trade could cut and slaughter prices as it liked. The tariff forbad all re-entry. In 1904, American material for steamship building was sold at Pittsburg at $32·00 a ton, at Belfast for $24·00. Connecticut watches sold for fifty cents in Syria— taking what the Arab had, no more. And meantime the huge growth of mechanical production and the constant application of inventions made wider and wider the difference between what the economists call " total costs " and " individual costs ", which latter means the extra cost of making one extra article when all the general apparatus is there already. This process grew into the " mass production " of America, beside which a lot of European manufactures begin to look like cottage industry.

Mass production was enormously accelerated by

the method which presently came to be called " standardization ". By this is meant the general regulation by the producer and the acceptance by the consumer of uniform standards, sizes, forms and materials. Vast quantities of articles are turned out, the separate parts of each of which can be used for any of the others. There are as few varieties as possible, as little diversity as human taste will allow. The result in the saving of economic costs is enormous. Machinery can be utilized to an ever-greater degree. There is little fear of overstocking any particular variety. A wonderful technical accuracy cuts and grinds " adjustable parts " true to the ten-thousandth of an inch. Any wheel fits any axle ; any propeller goes on any shaft ; any cogged wheel slips in adjustably among its fellows. Concentration on a few lines helps research, experiment and improvement. The Federal Government co-operates. No less than thirty-three of its different branches act in concert with the American Engineering Standards Committee. State Governments, highway commissions, railway commissions and industrial commissions all take a hand. The movement extends outward, beyond the national frontier. Central and South America are being standardized. A Pan-American conference held at Lima, Peru, in 1925 was followed by a second Pan-American standardization conference at Washington in 1927, to which representatives from twelve Latin-American Republics came as guests. Where standardization has once stepped in, American imports follow as a natural result. In return, standardized coffee, cocoa and tropical fruits come back to pay for standardized motor-cars and harvesters.

Where standardization steps in, all products begin to look alike. All railways are alike. All cars are alike. All houses and buildings, as far as material goes, begin to look alike. Variety drops out. There used to be sixty-six kinds of paving-bricks in use in the United States. There are now five. There were, not long ago, 552 kinds of wire fencing. It is now cut to sixty-nine. There used to be sixty kinds of hospital bedsteads, forty-nine kinds of milk-bottles and twenty-nine sorts of milk-bottle caps. Now there are only four hospital bedsteads, nine milk-bottles and one, only, milk-bottle cap. There were 700 kinds of dining-car china-ware sold to American railways, now only 113.

.   .   .   .

Then came the moving picture. The scientific preparation for it was laid chiefly in other lands— in England, in France, a little everywhere. But the Americans first realized and developed its commercial properties. Everybody old enough re- calls the gasp of wonder that greeted the original moving pictures of 1895. Here were Italian cavalry actually jumping a fence! A train actually and visibly running at forty miles an hour! Then the gasp of wonder was succeeded by a sigh of dis- illusionment. After all, Italian cavalry jumping a fence in a picture looks very like Italian cavalry jumping anything else, and a picture of a train running at forty miles an hour looks very like a train running over the Canadian Pacific Railway at forty miles an hour. The moving picture, like the telephone and the telegraph, was, at the start, an economic failure. The Americans saved it. They taught it to tell a story ; trained it in its own wooden, mechanical tricks of hysterical pantomime ; got the eye of the public trained to a flickering flat surface and figures from ten to forty feet high ; and above all, they threw about it a great wealth of scenery, vast moving open spaces of forest, sea wealth and desert, for which the cloudless climate and the sunlit sea of California took the industry to its soft breast.

From it came a world industry and the Americans fell heir to it. They had earned it. We could have done it ourselves, but we were too slow.

Out of all this has arisen the large-scale industry and the export trade of the United States. The export trade is conducted on the original principle of an American farm. Never buy anything you can make at home. Sell cheap where you can't sell dear. Be content to take merely what they have got. Live on what you can't sell. Export sales made this system run at present (using the year ending June 1928) to about $5,000,000,000 a year. There is an item of $425,000,000 sales of motor-cars and accessories. Few ever come in. There is agricultural machinery, $102,000,000 ; electrical machinery $87,000,000 ; and industrial machinery $210,000,000.

The farmers get their share ; the wheat alone that they export represents, one year with another, a value of $200,000,000, and the rest of the agricultural products, fluctuating much in price, move around $2,000,000,000 a year. In return are bought the things that Providence has seen fit to deny to

American soil : a coffee bill averaging $300,000,000, cane sugar $250,000,000, and about $120,000,000 of manufactured goods of peculiar European and other varieties.

But the account does not balance : there is a difference—a so-called " favourable " balance of from $900,000,000 to a thousand million (an American billion) dollars a year. To make this even, there are the huge tourist bills for food and scenery, civility and servility in Europe. Vast quantities of foreign exchange cross the ocean for that. And in the end, when Europe can pay no more, the rest is " invested " in Europe ; in other words (stated in language of the farm), the Americans give Europe " time " for what it can't pay, and then charge interest.

Up till now this looks to be the greatest system of foreign trade ever devised. It is. But running all through the system is a fatal flaw like a concealed crack in cast metal. By this at any time it may be smashed asunder. The system is too absolute, too exclusive. It is too complete. The protection is riveted and clamped as closely as an American steel frame. The industrial classes are so tightly organized that none will give way. There is nothing to concede, nothing to bargain with. The farmers are too powerful to be the victims of cheap grain and meat from Argentina. The steel-makers are too strong to permit the Government to let in anything from Birmingham or Essen. Every interest too powerful to allow foreign intrusion, every interest balanced, taut, is held in the rigid strain of its industrial setting. Touch one and you destroy all.

There is not one that can, that will, that dare concede anything.

And over against this is the glorious, the wonderful, the unused weapon of the non-existent tariff of Great Britain.

.   .   .   .

Now let us see where the friendly jolt, as playful as the McKinley tariff or the Hawley-Smoot Bill, may be given to the American colossus.

.   .   .   .

Here is Argentina, a vast country of 1,153,119 square miles of river valley and rolling prairie, of sunlit hill-sides—a natural paradise for field and farm production. It is overwhelmingly agricultural. Beef walks in the grass, finding its own food. Transport, cheap and easy, rolls over the level savannahs or floats on the broad network of rivers. Uncounted cattle, living or frozen, pass down the River Plate to the markets of Europe ; millions of bushels of grain seek each year the export market. But in return Argentina cannot manufacture. There is no coal or iron sufficiently available, no copper, no rubber, no trained mechanical population. Argentina is the natural partner, the bride, as it were, of some bold industrial country of the north. Observe what happens.

Argentina raises vast quantities of wheat, a crop of some six to eight million metric tons a year. The United States doesn't buy it. The tariff shuts it out. England buys about $50,000,000 worth of it every year. The Argentine, as no other country in the world, raises cattle. It kills and freezes about 5,000,000 cattle and 5,000,000 sheep every year. The United States won't buy them. Treating the Argentine peso as a dollar (it is within three and a half cents of one), we find that in the year 1928 (the last reported) the Argentine sold $111,000,000 worth of frozen or chilled meat, of which England bought $100,000,000. England has each year with Argentine a butcher's bill for meat, grain and produce of about $350,000,000. The United States refuses to deal at the shop.

There is no need to cumulate illustrations. The point is clear. Argentina depends for its economic life on the English market ; without it, there would be no tango in Buenos Ayres. But when it comes to buying, Argentina buys a little everywhere, and overwhelmingly from the United States. In 1928 Argentina bought from England $1,362,000 worth of oil and from the United States $51,528,000 ; bought from England in iron and steel $28,453,000 and from the United States $50,128,000 ; farm instruments from England $609,000, and from the United States $12,635,000. Most striking of all are the figures for the sale of motor-cars and motor-trucks. Here one could almost drop into poetry and say, " If you have tears, prepare to shed them now." In the year 1927 (last year reported) the Argentine bought from England $817,000 worth of motors and trucks and from the United States $25,693,000. Surely no one can look at that plain statement of fact and not see that something ought to be done about British export trade in manufactures. And if it is really true that a readjustment of the British tariff could give to England that whole market, duty free, while the United States would have to face the hostile tariff, is it not worth while at least to think about it ? Why allow a worn-out shibboleth to undermine the policy of a nation ? Why read economics only in a graveyard ?

.   .   .   .

The plain truth is that, apart from textiles and glassware, England has no real hold on the Argentine market. Now England could alter all this at a day's notice. Argentina has a tariff of almost the whole range of its imported goods ; and this tariff is just the same for England as the United States. At present there is no reason to make it different. But suppose that England said to the Argentine, " You will reduce your tariff in our favour by cutting it fifty per cent and we will do the same." Or better still, " If you will remove your tariff altogether, so will we." But alas ! England has no tariff in respect of its Argentine imports to cut or to reduce. When the market is free for all there are no favours to grant. Everywhere Great Britain is unable to make a reciprocal tariff bargain because there is no British tariff to bargain with. The compact made in 1929 on a small range of trade was excellent as a gesture. But since there is no British tariff anyway on the chief products of Argentina, it was only a gesture.

But suppose that England *did* have a tariff on wheat and meat and cattle and all such and removed it for Argentina, then it could get concessions in return as a *quid pro quo* that would give it the whole market. At present there is a *quid* but no *quo*. And notice that after the bargain had been made and finished and was in operation, Argentina wheat, grain and meat would come into England just as cheaply as ever.

It might be answered that the United States would follow suit and give the same preference. It can't. The American farmer wouldn't let it. There are 27,000,000 people in the farming class in the United States. Even now they think they can't live, or can't live as a farmer ought to do, with a car in the garage and a radio in the parlour. Suggest to them that Argentina food is coming in without a duty to compete in their market and they would reach, quite literally, a state bordering on mania.

.   .   .   .

Now instead of speaking of Argentina speak of all the world. Argentina is an extreme case. The same situation to a greater or less degree is reproduced all over the world. England cannot bargain.

But let us suppose, just for the sake of argument, that a tariff of fifteen per cent was imposed all round the British Empire. Imagine it to enclose the whole area, running along over the top of any existing tariff, like a Chinese wall over a hill, so that where Australia or Canada has an existing tariff of thirty or forty per cent on such and such an article, then the tariff on that article would be left just as it is, as far as the Empire is concerned, but raised to forty-five and fifty-five per cent as against the foreign world. And imagine that any tariff unit of the Empire—Great Britain, the Irish Free State, Canada, etc.—would be perfectly free to raise or lower, alter or abolish this extra tariff just as it liked. So that it would have something to use as a basis for reciprocal integral trade within the Empire. Then it could bargain and bargain with tremendous effectiveness.

Let it be observed at once that there is no particular virtue about fifteen per cent. It is necessary to start somewhere. And in the light of experience, fifteen per cent is enough to give a certain protection without reaching an extreme. It is equally clear that in the course of a very short time the simple symmetry of the fifteen per cent would be marred by all kinds of exceptions and modifications—just as happens with any protective tariff system at present. But it would be much easier to make a start on a simple ground plan of a super-tariff of fifteen per cent, and then let the exceptions come in their place, than to try all at once to frame, with the consent of seven different tariff authorities, the complete and complicated structure of an Empire reciprocal protective system.

Such a proposal is no sooner made than obvious objections to it occur so fast, that it is impossible to meet them all in one breath. It will be said at once that the whole thing is contrary to the principles of free trade. For many reverent minds in England that is enough, and this objection carries with it such a dead weight of authority, history, prejudice and prestige that it is well to deal with it first of all. It would not be possible in this place to examine in detail the economic system which began with Adam Smith in the *Wealth of Nations* of 1776, which was carried forward by Ricardo and other disciples after the Napoleonic War, which was set before the public by the inspired campaign of the Cobdens and

Brights of the Anti-Corn Law League, and which was triumphantly restated by John Stuart Mill in 1848.

This " system of natural liberty ", as its founder called it, swept the field. Trade was only a part of it. It meant freedom to buy and sell as one liked, with no one to interfere with the buyer and the seller ; to employ labour and to be employed as a labourer with no let or hindrance to the free bargain between the master and the man. Such things as the hours of labour and the conditions of labour, such questions as to whether women and children should work in factories and for how long they would work each day—all this was left to the free bargain made between the employer and the employee. Under it free children of nine years old worked twelve and fourteen hours a day, were carried to the factory by workless fathers in the dark of the morning and carried home exhausted at night. Anybody who does not know that this was one resulting aspect of the " system of natural liberty " does not know economic history. He may read it all in the famous report of the Factory Commission of 1833. To any parent's heart there is no more terrible page in industrial history. When the voice of the children at last reached the world it was the economic doctrine of industrial liberty that served as a bulwark of resistance against the passage of a factory law. All students know of the opposition of Senior and other economists to interference : John Stuart Mill— a human being first and an economist afterwards— weakened. But John Bright, sturdy fellow, hung out for the right to manage his own factories as he liked.

All this chapter of English history has drifted into the shadows of retrospect. A sort of conspiracy of silence surrounds it. People agree to forget that this wonderful freedom of the working child was one part of a "system of natural liberty", of which free trade was another. The two hung together. A convenient forgetfulness has pushed them apart.

. . . .

The trade side of the argument was simple to state and easy to understand. The late Lord Balfour was once reported as saying (in the Chamberlain days) that it could all be written out on half a sheet of note-paper. One might almost ask, why so much paper as all that ? The argument ran thus : In any country there are at any time just such and such a number of workers and no more ; there is just such and such an amount of capital (machinery, appliances, materials) and no more. Therefore the wisest road to wealth is to set the people to work at whatever thing is best suited to their country, its resources, its climate, its labour. Don't grow grapes under glass in England to make wine. Buy them in France and sell to the French something, such as rails or cutlery, which England can make best. Thus production distributes itself all over the world along the lines of the greatest productiveness. Let France produce its genial wine to cheer the weary manufacturer. Let the United States raise tobacco and raw cotton and wheat ; let Canada produce timber and let Iceland export its ice. This may not make a perfect world, but at least a world as nearly perfect as we can get. This may not make high wages for the workman, but it will at least make

wages as high as economic laws allow them to be.
Best of all, under this system there is no room left
for quarrels. Each nation helps the other. There
is no need for rival seizing of territory. All the world
belongs to everybody. Colonies drift off to independence and national boundaries are washed out
in the milk of universal love.

No more beautiful dream of the future was ever
dreamed outside of Shanghai.

.   .   .   .

And the argument about trade—not about war
—is all quite true and undeniable if we accept the
premises and face the conclusions. Now in Cobden's
days the conclusions happened to be just what
England wanted. It meant that England would
manufacture for all the world, and the rest of the
world would raise produce, or curiosities, or tropical
spices. The doctrine was absolutely cosmopolitan.
It meant that people would migrate to whatever
part of the world offered them the most favoured
living. Cobden was willing that they should. In
his lifetime about 3,600,000 people migrated from
Britain to the United States. He thought this
excellent and warmly recommended the inclusion
of Canada in the American Republic. But since
Cobden's day the whole basis of industry and export
has been altered. The advent of large scale
machinery and mass production has introduced the
newer aspect of costs never dreamed of by Smith,
Ricardo and the rest. What is the *cost* of one
American mowing machine ? How long can you
sell it in Argentina before you strike rock-bottom
and can go no lower ? You can disregard all the

cost of the initial establishment of the industry, all the factory building and machine buying, all the clerical cost and the overhead cost and the advertising cost—and as far as that one single sale of that one single machine is concerned, you can sell it in Argentina (if you can get no better price) for anything over the bare cost of the few bits of stick and iron that are in it, and the water transport that brought it. What is this ? Something down nearly to nothing. In practice you don't sell it at that. That is merely the zero mark on the thermometer. You sell it at any better price which the market allows.

The average costs of all the machines averaged over the whole industry—the thing that the Ricardos and the Mills called the " cost " is only an arithmetical expression. If the business can't get this it will fail. But it will take as much more as it will get : and sell any single article, when once made, clean down to the zero mark if it can do no better. More than that ; unless its plant is running to the full on higher prices it will deliberately make extra goods to sell low if they won't sell high. The overhead costs are there, anyway : if the goods made and sold cheap won't cover them all, they will at least cover part of them. This is the great outstanding problem of export prices, of " dumping " and the slaughter market. It is just here that the United States with its vast mass production, its machinery, its standardized output and its quick ingenious brains, stands triumphant in world manufacture.

We emphasize the brains. The United States was the first country to discover that business was respectable, and to throw its best brains into the front line of the industrial advance. The English know now as well as we do on this continent that the big business of large manufacture is vast, absorbing, creative. But they were long in learning it. For generations they tried to keep to the idea, inherited from Greece, that trade was low ; that the real work of brains was to read over the Greek orations two or three times a year, and to take a little sip of Latin poetry before bedtime.

In other words, the whole setting of Cobden's world has changed. Whether he liked it or not, the other nations refused to accept their parts in distributed production. They refused to be altogether agricultural, or altogether mineral, or altogether anything. Manufacture meant cities, and cities meant opportunity and intercourse and culture and stimulated national life. The nations wanted to manufacture ; and did. One by one they accepted national permanent protection—the United States, then France and finally Germany. The ungrateful colonies, Canada and Victoria, had been among the first to go. All the world knows that.

The Cobdenite answer was quite simple. One tariff is bad, but two would make it worse. So free trade went on. But the other forces refused to be set at naught. Free trade means international migration. Your people leave home to build up foreign countries. Cobden didn't mind. We do. He said that as there would be no war citizenship doesn't matter. We know it does. In the last count the greatest asset of a nation is its population.

Last comes the crushing weight of the export trade

situation. The nation that keeps its own market can overwhelm the others. There is no answer to it. This is the final staggering blow that will kill free trade.

.   .   .   .

It might be said that in all that has gone above the consumer has been left out of count. He has, quite purposely.

In all the earlier economic discussions of free trade there appeared the domineering and disagreeable personality of the " consumer ". His interests formed a leading consideration in the discussion of economic policy.

The business of this imaginary person was to consume : he ate corn, wore out clothes, consumed —like a worm in the wood—even pianos, carriages, and houses. And this was all that he did. He had no work, no business, no job. He knew nothing of good times or bad, of steady work or unemployment, of large profits or small, little dividends or big. It was all one to him. He just *consumed*.

It is time now for some one to make the economic discovery that the consumer does not exist. There is no such person.

In real life each one of us is not so much interested in the cheapness or dearness of things as in our chance of having the money to buy them. The average man thinks in terms of his salary, or his wages, of the profits that he is expecting to make, or fearing to lose. He shudders at the fear that he may " get the sack " or that slack times may turn him out of work for the winter. He dreams of an increase of salary, of a substantial " bonus " at

Christmas, of regular work at a "swell job" at high pay, or of a stock dividend added to his profits.

But does he stick his nose into a Government Blue-Book to see whether the current index of the purchasing power of money is rising or falling ? Never. Most likely he doesn't know what it is.

It will be said at once that people who live on "fixed incomes" are consumers. If it is said, it is wrong. The statement was more or less true in the days when there were fixed incomes. But now there are none left. In the world in which we live there is not an income that may not be affected—raised or lowered, interrupted or annihilated—by the changing circumstances of production and the changing prosperity of the country.

Take the shareholders of the industrial companies whose investments vastly overtop the money invested in Government securities. Every one of the shareholders is a producer in the fullest sense of the term. His main interest is in the business, not in the prices he pays for what he eats and drinks. If the business fails he will eat and drink no more. Take even the bond-holders. They too are interested in what is happening to production. The capital value of their bonds rises and falls. Even bonds, as many people know to their cost, can fail of their interest, and collapse to a complete loss. In fact, bonds can no more go on paying interest and redeeming capital without work, wealth and prosperity than stocks and shares can. The bond-holder is a producer, by proxy.

Take lastly the annuitants. Here is a country clergyman with a "living" worth £400 a year ;

here is a spinster in a Devonshire village with an income from Consols of £100. Surely these would seem consumers? No, they are not. They once were—in the days when England did not owe £8,000,000,000, when there had been no Great War and no one could imagine one, and when the land and the livings and the fixed incomes and the social structure of England seemed as firm as the rock on which the island rested. Not so now. If times are bad enough, and life for the workers hard enough, overboard goes the national debt and the livings and the vicar and the spinster and all the rest of it. These people, like all the rest of us, are not consumers. What they want, what they need, is prosperity, prosperity, prosperity.

. . . .

But even supposing that we take the consumer on his own terms and at his own querulousness. How much will he have to cry about? To what extent would an Empire tariff of, let us say, fifteen per cent be felt by him.

Take the case of *bread*, the focus-point of argument and the source of anger and tears since the days when Ebenezer Elliott wrote in his *Corn Law Rhymes*:

> *Child is thy father dead*
> *Father is gone:*
> *Why did they tax his bread*
> *Food we have none.*

So wept Ebenezer in 1840. And in those days they did tax " Father's bread ", and taxed it good and proper. Under the law of 1815 no wheat could come in from abroad unless the home price was at least 80 shillings a quarter—$2·50 a bushel. Even at that, the price rose in 1817 to 117 shillings ($3·65 a bushel). In Adam Smith's time a gallon loaf of bread (eight pounds eleven ounces) cost from one shilling to one and sixpence or four cents a pound, and eighteenth-century wages were so regulated by the Justices of the Peace that a " poor and industrious man " should have the value of three of these loaves a week for himself and one and a half for each child. His day's wage was equal to four pounds of bread, or sixpence. So when Ebenezer Elliott cried he had something to cry for, and when he asked why did they tax father's bread, the answer should have been that they taxed father's bread because they hoped to make large incomes for British landholders, and to do it they had to take it from father. The brutality of this has coloured the whole historic controversy. But the original picture of father dying from the *ad valorem* tariff and mother selling her bed, for reasons not clear in the poem, has about as much to do with the situation to-day as have the Crusades and Inquisition or the execution of Mary Queen of Scots.

Let us look at the case as it is to-day. Cut all the sentimentality out of it and state it in cold terms of business. England grows at present each year 50,000,000 bushels of wheat. It imports about 200,000,000 bushels, or, using the figures of the year 1928, let us say, 191,000,000 bushels. Of this, one-half came from within the Empire and one-half from foreign countries. Canada supplied 76,000,000 bushels, the United States 43,000,000, Argentina 44,000,000, and Australia 18,000,000 bushels.

Out of this bread is made. A "quartern" loaf of bread in London weighs four pounds. The wheat in it at a Liverpool price of eight shillings per English hundredweight is worth about 8·8 cents, or fourpence three farthings. The common and average selling price of the quartern loaf is ninepence, or twopence one farthing per pound. It is evident, then, that not only wheat makes the loaf, but the grinding of the wheat into flour and the labour of making the bread, transporting it and selling it. Note that in the world in which we live the cost of selling things is rapidly surpassing the cost of making them. Even so plain a necessity as bread needs a certain amount of wrapping and display and shouting to sell it— apart from the cost of carrying it around. In the case of the bread, almost one-half of its value represents the labour of the miller, the baker and the shopkeeper. What the consumer holds, there- fore, when he sits weeping over his sixteen-ounce loaf, the ordinary pound of bread, is about three cents' worth of wheat. If you put a tariff of fifteen per cent on the incoming foreign wheat, and not on the colonial wheat, how will this affect the price of the loaf ? The answer is that you wouldn't know it was there. If the tax covered *all* the wheat con- sumed, every grain of it, British, Colonial and foreign, and if all the fifteen per cent, the whole of it, was shifted on to the consumer (it wouldn't be, not all of it, but suppose it was ; in short, suppose that each of all of these extreme assumptions were true), then the price of the loaf would rise by fifteen per cent of the cost of the wheat—that is, by not quite a halfpenny. But if there is no tax on the

British wheat, none on the Canadian wheat, and none, on a reciprocal system, on the Argentine wheat —in other words, no tax on two-thirds of the import —then the price won't rise one farthing. Dry your tears, Ebenezer, Father can still be fed.

One might ask, then, how the imposition of this duty on foreign wheat, which would be imperceptible to the London consumer, would be of great importance to the Saskatchewan producer. The reason is this. The Saskatchewan farmer is producing wheat all day every day. That is, directly and indirectly, his sole occupation. Hence, a very slight difference in the price per bushel means a lot to him. But the consumer does not sit and chew bread all day. If he did this, if he really sat and ate bread from morning to night, loaf after loaf, then the slightest rise in price, the tenth of a farthing, would make a lot of difference. But as eating bread is only a small part of his existence the case is altered.

With the farmer in Saskatchewan even a fifteen per cent duty in his favour will mean a real benefit. He gets the *market*. The American can only sell by sacrificing anything from fifteen to twenty-one cents a bushel on a price from a dollar to a dollar and a half. Wheat-growing in consequence falls off in the States, and wheat-growing and wheat-land and settlement flourishes in the Canadian West. The people pour into the new wheat-fields, and with them capital and transport and all the mechanism of cultural civilization. So does a little impetus give momentum to a mass almost willing to move.

. . . .

A sagacious person might object that there is a

decidedly weak spot in this argument. What about all this Argentina wheat coming into England on even terms with the Canadian. Where does Canada stand on that ? That seems at first sight allowing the foreigner to share in the preferential benefit given to the Dominions. But this is only true if we isolate that one fact of Empire trade without considering its setting. It ceases to be true when we really grasp the idea of an integrated tariff system. What the foreigner gains in one direction he pays for in another. Under the arrangement proposed, the tariff privilege given to Great Britain to send manufactured goods into Argentina on better terms than those given to the United States extends, of course, to Canada and the other Dominions. It applies to the agricultural machinery made in Canada and just like the American, to the motor-cars of Oshawa and Windsor, the electric apparatus of the great Canadian electrical companies—in other words, there is a $400,000,000 market thrown open to the manufacturers of Canada, Australia and the Empire to divide.

Under such terms can they get it ? Can they take it from the Americans even then ? They certainly can, as far as the tariff goes. The United States can never sacrifice its mournful farmers. Ever since the agricultural tariff of 1895 the Government has done all it could for them. It has protected every-thing they grow from hops to hogs. It has built them roads and taken away the rye whisky that was tearing the stomachs out of them. And they are mournful still. They now want the Government to shovel away the St. Lawrence River, so that the sea can come to them. Imagine telling this class (27,000,000 people) that Argentina grain is coming in without a duty!

But even at that are the Americans beaten? Perhaps not. The enormous mass-production of the United States, the standardization of its goods, and its perpetual application of mechanical principles to new processes might still enable it to leap over a tariff wall and carry slaughter with it. Where they could not get a dollar in Argentina the Americans would take eighty cents; and if not eighty, sixty, and so on down to the rock-bottom cost that alone stops export sale.

The only answer to this is to beat the Americans at their own game. If we can't do that we deserve to lose. We must reorganize the manufacturing industries of the Empire so that they can compete on even terms with those of the American Republic, and easily beat it where we enjoy a tariff privilege under an integrated imperial system. If they can standardize so can we; if they can produce in the mass, so can we; if they can apply scientific research to large scale industry, so can we; and when it come to the sheer wealth of raw materials we have their little country beaten at the start.

To do this we must in the American phrase " get together ". To do this we have to bring our imperial manufacturing system into far less of conflict and far more of harmony than it is now.

This does not mean that we could for a moment remove the protective system which surrounds and fosters the greater industries of Canada and Australia and the rest. This is not possible. Whether or not it was wise, forty years ago, to call protected industries into being is now a purely academic question. It can be left to the professors. And these do not agree. But the industries are there ; they represent an enormous equipment of physical plant and monetary investment. They have helped to bring about an urban concentration in the great Dominions that could not have come without them and could not continue without them. But owing to the circumstances and conditions under which they operate, their costs, especially in labour, are higher than in Great Britain. Remove the tariff and they fall. With their fall they bring down in a struggling mass whole cities of traders, lawyers, hotel keepers, actors, artists, clergymen, university professors, political economists—in short, all that unhappy class who crowd our cities, whom Ricardo and Mill called unproductive, whom the Socialists call parasitic, but whose existence cannot be disregarded.

. . . .

But an enormous amount can be done by way of connecting and combining British and Dominion manufacture, British and Dominion capital and British and Dominion labour, technique, research and industrial science. It is not possible in this place to do more than indicate the field that can be occupied.

A standardization of processes, methods and machines—of weights, quantities, packages—of sizes, grades, boxes, bottles and containers—in short, of the whole apparatus and mechanism of manufacture—would enormously benefit all parts of the Empire. There ought to be, as explained in a later chapter, a unification of money, weights and measures. The British cling to their pound sterling with its primitive and impossible subdivisions. We can continue to live with it, but it is a hindrance and helps to divide and differentiate our common commercial life. At present our manufacturers are groups of enemies, or at least of suspicious acquaintances. British capital is not invested as American capital is, in branch factories and branch establishments. As shown elsewhere in this book British capital clings to old maids' investments in dead-safe bonds at fixed interest, while American capital, joining in Canadian enterprise, takes an adventurous chance.

There is no reason why a protected industry in Australia and Canada should not " merge " with a British industry. They would all gain power thereby and all act together to secure the foreign markets. As an initial step they must, of course, be protected by an Empire super-tariff, running all round the Empire, adjustable and flexible, and used as the basis of reciprocal dealings with the outside world. To examine the details of such a tariff is far beyond the purpose of this book. That would require a congress of trade experts, working upon a wilderness of facts and figures, and producing a report that would be read only by those who could not avoid reading it.

But the general idea, as outlined above, is one that can be understood and judged by anybody. If the idea is worthless the details are not needed. If the idea is sound the details are only a matter of patient industry.

CHAPTER II

A PROPOSAL OF POLICY FOR THE SETTLE-
MENT OF NEW COUNTRY

THE first part of this book was intended to set forth certain large facts. It appeared that the great Dominions of the temperate zones possess basic resources that could maintain, easily and beyond all question, half a billion people. Now there is in Great Britain an immediate surplus population—or, at least, if the word surplus is offensive—a population disposable for migration, of some 2,000,000 people. There is also, if happier circumstances restored the British birth-rate to its normal function, the basis for an annual outflow of population amounting to perhaps 2,000,000 people. The white population of the Dominions also, if permitted its natural increase, would represent an annual addition of about half as much. Here then is a vast open land, and a great fund of people. With this is also in existence a mechanism of transport which would make the mere physical removal of the population four or five thousand miles a simple task. There is in existence, moreover, a great fund of capital goods, machines and factories, and machines for making other machines, and factories making material to build factories—so great that we cannot find work for it to do, and that the economic line of effort is no longer to produce but to sell. If this capital is converted into terms of money, we have seen that Great Britain up to the war-time had exported about £4,000,000,000 worth of capital, and even now could contribute capital to the extent of from £100,000,000 to £200,000,000 worth every year, if means were found for its application. More than that, the outside world and especially the United States has an accumulation and increasing supply of capital goods available for the development of countries other than its own. This represents, in the case of the United States, at least, $2,000,000,000 every year. Here are the factors of the situation, the land, the people, the capital—plenty of all of them. The problem is how are we to bring them together. What we have to examine is the economic problem of the settlement of an empty country. It ought to be a part of what is recognized as the modern theory of political economy. So far as I know it is not. It stays exactly where Gibbon Wakefield and the " systematic colonizers " laid it down nearly a century ago.

. . . .

In stepping out on this ground we enter on a field of controversy. This is especially so if one proposes, as I do, to outline a particular concrete plan as to what can be done. I cannot hope to find in this a unanimous consent or anything like it among those who may read this book. With the general aspiration towards Imperial prosperity most readers will be in warm sympathy, else they would not read. But when it comes to definite proposals and particular plans, dissent and division of opinion are inevitable. Against which I can only repeat what has been said above, that if this book has value it lies rather in its general plan of integration than in the suggestion of any one particular detail in carrying it out.

．　．　．　．　．　．　．　．　．

One may begin with a few very simple generalities that take us back to Robinson Crusoe and the Swiss Family Robinson. Suppose that a group of human beings without food, or capital, appliances or outside contacts were set down upon an isolated territory of barren rock they could not live. Nor would it make any difference if the barren rock were made of nickel and cobalt. If the same group of people, or any one or more of them, were set down in a fertile and favoured country, even without tools and appliances, they might survive and slowly advance towards an industrial civilization. But for this there would be needed a climate, or a season, mild enough to let them dispense with houses, an abundance of natural fruits and accommodating game—a set of circumstances found only in the pages of romance in some murmuring island of the South Seas.

But if a community of human beings can be placed in an unoccupied and fertile land, with arable soil, forests, and fisheries and mineral wealth, and if they can bring with them the whole material apparatus of production and transport, and initial food and shelter for their period of probation, then the case is entirely different. Their removal from their older habitation makes, of course, a heavy draft upon the accumulated stock of the country from which they come. All the food, machinery, and equipment that they bring must come out of the fruit of the labour of the past. Their numbers and their movement are therefore at once conditioned by the surplus wealth and numbers of their time and place of origin. Elizabethan England could not have sent out a million people equipped to reach and occupy the fertile prairies of North America, even had they dreamed of doing so. Modern England could do easily as much at any time. It is to be noticed, however, that in a fertile territory the work of the new-comers very soon begins to result in an industrial surplus (measured over the crowd, not of necessity for each single person). With this surplus they can carry their settlement further : or they can begin to pay back in produce and goods the initial advances made to them. The million people mentioned above could easily pay back to England all the advance necessities of their migration, and plenty of interest on it. As their numbers and wealth increased they could arrange for further immigration with their own industrial surplus. Under present circumstances fertile territory possessed of basic resources does not need to wait, as it used to, to be settled man by man. It could be done now in the lump, as a single operation of capitalistic finance. Southern Ontario, if it had its forests back again, need not have been cleared by the axe of the pioneer. It could have been cleared by the large-scale machinery of a timber corporation financed from England.

.   .   .   .

One pauses a moment at the heroic figure of the pioneer, the man with the axe. His achievement still illuminates our history, and misleads our public policy. In the eighteenth and early nineteenth century, individual pioneer settlement was the only available means of exploiting empty country. But we should not carry it over into the twentieth century, where it ought to be as antiquated as the spinning wheel and the horse pistol. The pioneer, in the day that is now, belongs only in a museum, or at best in a self-elected skirmish line beyond the main advance of civilization. For the main problem of Empire settlement the lonely effort of the pioneer in his log cabin, with his coon-skins and his shot guns, has nothing to say.

Till nearly the middle of the nineteenth century the limitations of transport and available capital rendered individual settlement the only one in the field. Hence British migration had to direct itself towards territory of a distinctive character, a territory of resources immediately and directly available. I am not here speaking of the expansion that was purely a matter of commerce, as when British traders entered the harbours of India or Ceylon ; nor of predatory and commercial slave-catching in Africa ; nor gold and treasure hunting anywhere and everywhere. The reference is to the making of new homes in the land as, typically, the settlement of North America. Here for a bare and simple livelihood no great start was needed, no great stock of capital goods : transport across the sea ; food for a few months ; a stock of tools with the inevitable axe as the very symbol of conquest ; a spinning-wheel ; a bible and a few books.

The United Empire Loyalists and those who followed them into Upper Canada were, some of them, people of substance who brought with them a fair amount of property. But it was not necessary. Others came with nothing more than the value of one year's food. That sufficed. By this pioneer process, almost exclusively, the Atlantic slope of North America was first settled. The French, perhaps, had larger ideas ; but their people were not migratory, and the large ideas of the Hundred Associates and such failed of effect. The Virginia Company's first attempt at collective and co-operative settlement, Penn's proprietary colony and later Lord Selkirk's colony of 1820 on the Red River all dissolved into pioneerism. In the limited circumstances of the time it answered its purpose. America was mainly settled, man by man, and axe by axe. But the process was slow. It took 200 years—from Raleigh's abortive colony till the constitution of 1789—to establish three and a half million white people in North America. That, for us, is too slow.

But this process of settlement left a deep furrow in public policy corresponding to a deep fold in public opinion. We still think of the settlement of a new country as something done by the single man, by his single effort. The Canadian homestead law (first adopted in 1872) started from that, and is based on a historical misconception. Land settlement to-day is exactly what the single man, acting singly, cannot achieve. If he had the money to do it, he would probably not want to do it. To offer an empty-handed man in Glasgow a homestead in Saskatchewan is only a joke. The problem of land settlement now must start from an entirely different point of view. It involves a vast quantity of capital, and a great force of co-ordinated labour.

. . . .

In other words, it is only in rare circumstances that, unaided, the individual man, " the man with the axe ", migrates into new empty territory and makes a living from the start. The achievement of the Swiss Family Robinson, of Robinson Crusoe and of Jules Verne's scientific castaways are romantic and appealing. But they belong only to a desert island equipped like a departmental store. The migration of the man with the axe may be left out of count as a solution of the present Imperial problem.

Even such a system as the homestead plan falls far short of the present situation. It demands a special territory, the existence of a special market, and, above all, special people to make it good. The American settlers of the " invasion " of 1905–1913 fitted into the plan to a nicety. They were trained in the knowledge needed. They brought the property and capital needed for a start. And they came at a time when the production of the single commodity wheat still found a market which might vary somewhat but could not entirely fail. The day for all that is past. Migration and settlement must be carried on now as part of a huge co-operative capitalistic plan.

. . . .

I say capitalistic to indicate that I do not mean socialistic. What is needed is the collective, corporate use of capital, bringing with it the incentive of private gain. There are, no doubt, many people

186

who would agree with me that migration must be done on a large plan and with a basis of equipment, but would see in it therefore an operation to be carried through on Socialist lines. For quickness' sake I hope to part company at once with readers who think in terms of Socialism. I do not think that anything but failure could come from socialistic schemes of migration and settlement in which the " state " becomes the moving power and the sole owner of the land and the means of production. This is as futile as all the rest of Socialism—a noble aspiration fit for the Kingdom of Heaven, where it would work without compulsion, or for Hades, where it is probably in operation already.

In my opinion, reliance can only be placed on individual self-interest and individual gain as the motive power of economic action.

But, it may be said, even without going to the final length socialism, the whole affair of large scale migration and land settlement might be carried out as a Government enterprise. Such is the typical point of view of the sentimental theorist, or the youthful member of the intelligentsia who has as yet no money, no property to pledge, no savings to lose, and no great love of work for its own sake. In his mind he creates an abstraction called the Government, which represents a sort of fairy godmother or wealthy uncle. Such people can form the easy imaginary picture of a government, arranging transport, with exquisite efficiency, engaging a multitude of officials (on a pure basis of capacity), paying salaries (without intrigue or favour), buying materials for houses (at severely competitive prices), appointing superintendents (the best men), and starting industries, selling products and planning new openings, always with keen, unflagging zeal, without ineptitude or crookedness. Such a picture is just a dream : fit only for a fairy-book.

The experience of a hundred years of democracy has shown us what a Government can do and what not. Some things it does well, some very badly, some not at all. In a matter of pure routine where eager initiative counts for little or nothing, governmental activity is excellent. The Government keeps track of the weather marvellously well. It collects statistics, makes surveys and measures the depths of the sea, with quiet unvarying efficiency. Perhaps it even runs a post office better than free private enterprise could do. Where private incentive is feeble, as in educating other people's children, or private forethought indifferent and careless as in public health, Government steps in to do what others would leave undone. A Government is excellent, too, in its generosity towards scholarship, research, science and discovery. In short, the Government is an excellent grandmother.

More than that. It may be that in certain economic functions which can be reduced to a regular and standardized set of services, governmental operation can compete with private enterprise. The matter of transportation might be considered by many an open question. But when it comes to large scale business enterprise expected to result in a definite reproductive return, measurable in pounds, shillings, and pence and in dollars and cents, the Government is nowhere. As soon as it steps into

economic work of this kind, it spills money like a
drunken sailor at a fair. Salaries are paid by
favour ; contracts are made for love ; and supplies
are bought for good fellowship. There is no Argus
eye to watch expenditure. There is no shareholder
to placate. There is no bankruptcy to fear.

This is not altogether to the discredit of the
Government. It means, in a way, that the Govern-
ment is too decent to be in business. It brings to
bear that private kindliness of feeling which each
of us would like to exercise, but dares not. The
Government hates to " fire anybody " : and doesn't.
The employer hates to fire anybody : and does.
That's all the difference ; but it is a lot.

To ask, then, the British and the Dominion
Governments to embark four or five billion dollars
on a State-owned, large-scale scheme of migration
and development would only end in disaster. The
process would create a temporary onrush of activity,
prosperity and work for all, followed by a dead
collapse and a downhill slide towards bankruptcy.

. . . .

Now no individual fortune is ample enough for
the whole undertaking in question. The obvious
recourse is to corporate enterprise. Migration and
development should be carried on as a large corporate
undertaking in which a great many people venture
their capital in the hope of a solid financial gain.
Neither State-aid nor sentiment nor philanthropy
can do it alone. There are not enough Selkirks
among us for that. There is a limit to which any
reasonable taxpayer will want to go in defraying
out of Government money the cost of sending other

people's children to Tasmania and Saskatchewan. Imagine, then, a series of large corporations set on foot to develop the white man's empire and equipped by Great Britain and by the Dominions with all sorts of privileges, franchises, monopolies—with opportunities, in a word, calculated to call forth money in cartloads.

The mainspring of the whole mechanism is found in the individual investor. His eager acquisitive interest, his unchristian desire to get a lot for a little, is the motive power that keeps the economic world in movement. The history of British foreign investment as recited above has shown how keen this economic motive is. In the contemporary age the investor has penetrated, by proxy, into the frozen regions of the north, the rubber swamps of the jungle and the deserts of the equator. Behind the aviator as he makes an exploration flight over the mineral wildernesses of Canada there is seated, though visible only to the eye of the imagination, the prosaic little figure of the investor, holding tight his hat in the fierce air current of the north. Deep in a coal mine you will find him, or pearl-fishing in a lagoon in the Southern Seas, or following after the " timber cruiser " to measure out board feet of lumber available in a silent forest of unbroken pine. What looks to the eye of romance to be the search for adventure, the charm of the great open spaces, is, in cold reality, the urge of the investor. The " mystery and beauty of the ships and the magic of the sea ", as Longfellow thought of it, is in our day the search for dividends. If biological theories of human development are well founded the process amply justifies itself. It represents humanity eagerly seeking the new forces and the ever-increasing control over Nature without which it cannot survive. But there is no need to appeal to either history or imagination to realize the force of the investment motive. Within the present post-War period it has shown itself more intensely than ever. Investment now arises not merely for the sake of savings and interest but from the more eager hope of capital gain through a rise in values. The New York stock market roars like the draught of a blast furnace. The fires may be damped for a moment, but not for long. Humanity has learned a form of excitement, a hope of success, which it will not henceforth relinquish. Fraud, failure, ruin will no more stop the recurrence of speculative investment than death stops the recurrence of war.

Nor is the investor altogether wrong. He wants a run for his money. Life is so drab, so quiet ; work so remorseless ; the end of it all so certain. The investor wants a run for his money before he dies. Let him have it. And in the development of the British Empire we could give him a good one. If Imperial incorporate companies of the kind I here propose were set on foot, the subscription books of shares would fill up in a day.

Let me attempt to explain in further detail what I mean by the companies themselves and what their operation would be and their relation to the emigrant and to natural resources. As I see it such companies would be under incorporation by the British and Dominion Governments in an associated capacity ; a new kind of incorporation ; an Imperial incorporation. The terms of subscription, the guarantees against fraud, the conditions of stock payment, the privileges granted and the obligations incurred would be by joint agreement with the associated Empire. For stability's sake, part of their bonded debt, if need be, could be under Imperial guarantee. The aim would be to grant honest fair conditions of incorporation, with a big chance for the shareholders and a dead certainty of employment and business for thousands of other people. Concession companies of this kind could be formed anywhere and everywhere in the Empire for purposes involving the development of resources and the settlement of population in new areas. Their financial basis would be the money of a myriad of investors, both inside the Empire and outside of it. The part played by the associated Government would be in arranging and legalizing the terms of the concessions and carrying on in all the new country the cost of certain services—surveys, telegraphs, and even to some extent roads, bridges and transport, all of which could be financed with reproductive governmental loans. If these loans were made a part of a pan-Imperial governmental debt, of which I shall speak in the next chapter, they could probably be floated at the lowest rates known to the financial world. Even the credit of the United States ought not to stand higher than that of a amalgamated British Imperial loan. Economic exploitation companies are already operating all over the world; there is a whole flock of them in Colombia and Venezuela seeking oil. They are penetrating Amazonian Brazil, and are prodding round in the

Garden of Eden looking for oil. But from the point of view of the development of the Empire they are mostly in the wrong place, doing the wrong thing. What we need to do is to connect up their eager economic driving power with the problem of Empire settlement. Innumerable examples of the field indicated might be taken from Australia, or New Zealand, or the Rhodesias, or other white man's territories of the Empire. But I prefer to show what I mean by illustrations taken from the Dominion of Canada. Imagine, if you will, a company receiving the exclusive fishing rights of the Hudson Bay and the mineral rights, the value of which there are already more than whispers, of the islands that lie in it ; or a concession to build a railway from James Bay via the Nottaway River to the transcontinental line as a winter outlet from the Hudson Bay with timber, mineral, and water-power rights as a consideration ; or to take over for agricultural settlement, and for timber, a section of that wonderful region, the last land of the sunset, the watershed drained by the Peace River ; to build a railway across Northern British Columbia from the Pacific Ocean at Prince Rupert to the junction of the Liard and the Fort Nelson River ; to exploit the oil resources of the Mackenzie basin, or the great copper deposits that most likely lie under the frozen soil and the treeless rock of the valley of the Coppermine River. Such things rise before the mind's eye with all the attraction of the unknown, the mystery of the wilderness, the lure of the unconquered. Economic, no doubt, it is, the urge, the driving power. But the element of romance is there as well. Companies of the sort described would have to undertake in return to employ and to settle—not necessarily on farms, but as workers—so many hundred or so many thousand, or so many hundred thousand workers and families, according to the scale and size of their concessions and operations. They could take some of their labour from the present over-supply of the Dominions, and such and such a fraction of it by migration (without cost to the emigrant) from Great Britain. It would of course be difficult to arrange the terms, the amount done by the Government of Great Britain, by the Dominion Government, by the provincial Government and by the concession company. But that is not a difficulty inherent in the undertaking. That is a difficulty which we have deliberately introduced into it by ninety years of careful subdivision of the Empire. But one could imagine a general act framed for acceptance at will by the Governments concerned, like the Empire Settlement Act of 1922 and the Naturalization Act of 1911. If a public opinion were formed around the idea, the parliamentary and legal mechanism would soon be found.

But it is to be noticed that there is one person concerned whose initial contribution is easily adjusted. That person is the landless, jobless emigrant, the man, on the " dole " in London or out of work in Montreal. His contribution is nothing. Therein lies the whole virtue and meaning of the plan.

. . . .

We must start, I say, from the fact that the emigrant, or local worker, with whom we are concerned possesses nothing ; or, more likely, in the form of a dependent wife and children, possesses, economically, less than nothing. We have to start from this. Any scheme of migration dealing with thrifty Scottish farmers who have saved a hundred pounds, or well-to-do Americans from Kansas, or young men whose people will pay a hundred pounds to get rid of them, is quite beside the mark.

The emigrant has nothing, except his capacity to work. If he is disabled and cannot work, his case lies outside of this book. But at present, let us say, he cannot find work ; he is one of the 2,000,000 unemployed and the 5,000,000 under-employed of Great Britain.

Citizens of alien countries are not under consideration, do not fit into the scheme. The outer empire needs population and settlement. Part of it, like Canada, can only carry its " overhead " of transportation and capital investment on the condition that a stream of new-comers shall move in. If there were no available British to come, we should very likely have to take in others or drift into liquidation. But it so happens that there are British—millions of them. The others we only need as a second-best choice.

Canada, especially in its north-west provinces, is badly damaged in this respect. As a result of the great foreign immigration before the War, the last census of Canada showed among its inhabitants 459,000 people born in continental Europe, including 57,000 Austrians, 31,000 Galicians, 101,000 Russians, 21,000 Poles, 35,000 Italians, and various others.

From the point of view of the Russians and the Galicians, etc., this meant improvement for the north-west. Not so from ours. Learning English and living under the British flag may make a British subject in the legal sense, but not in the real sense, in the light of national history and continuity. A few such people can easily be absorbed—over a large area many thousands can be absorbed. A little dose of them may even, by variation, do good, like a minute dose of poison in a medicine. But if you get enough of them, you get absorbed yourself. What you called the British Empire turns into the Russian and Galician Empire.

I am not saying that we should absolutely shut out and debar the European foreigner, as we should and do shut out the Oriental. But we should in no way facilitate his coming. Not for him the free ocean transit, nor the free coffee of the immigrant shed, nor the free land, nor the found job, nor the guaranteed anything. He is lucky if he is let in " on his own ".

But we come back to the penniless, able-bodied British immigrant and his dependants. Since the War the British unemployed have numbered anything from about 1,000,000 to 2,000,000. Even the accumulated wealth and the productive power of the country cannot continue indefinitely to support them. The recent British budgets carry a burden of some £370,000,000 as interest and charges on the national debt, a sum of over £50,000,000 as war pensions, a first claim on national gratitude and national resources, a sum of about £24,000,000 on non-contributory old-age pensions : sums paid out of local rates for the relief of the poor to a total of about £46,000,000 ; and the money paid to the unemployed in the eight years 1920-27 amounted in all to £303,000,000, or nearly £64,000,000 a year. Of this last item, it is true, £220,000,000 was collected from employers and workers under the Unemployed Insurance Act. But the social burden as a total is none the less. The dead weight of all this together is too much. Something has got to be done. And the only thing to be done is to turn the unemployed into productive workers. It is not likely that this can be done in England. It is doubtful whether the utmost impetus and stimulus of tariff change could pick up so heavy a weight and permanently carry it. The unemployed have got to go. And the outside empire, properly organized, needs them. The burden would turn into an asset. The word " man-power ", forgotten since the War, would get back its meaning.

Any and all of these people would migrate to the outer empire if they were given free transit and a job on arrival. If they wouldn't, it would be a fair proposal to suggest to them that they die of starvation.

Now if you take a man across the ocean and then merely dump him down, let us say, in north-west Canada and show him 160 acres of empty prairie and tell him that it is his, you have still done nothing for him. He can't use it ; indeed, he would die on it more quickly than he would in the slums of Glasgow, for here he is beyond the reach of charity and the casual penny. It is on this point that the homestead system has proved hopelessly inadequate.

Like so much in this world it has only meant that to those who have is given.

Equally ridiculous it would be to give to this landless man, free of cost, a farm, a house, a set of farm buildings, horses, machinery and supplies. This pretty little endowment, capitalized, would have just about kept him for life in Glasgow. Australian experience under the Empire Settlement Act proves as much. Nor can he receive and use all this equipment on the loan and long-payment system. He could never pay. He wouldn't know how to begin, what to do. The wealth so easily acquired would run away into the sand. Subsidized idleness would sit down on the job—defiant of ejection. For where could you eject him to ? Not to prison. Sentiment won't allow it. Back into the unemployed ? And then the chain begins again. And in any case, who would advance all the capital needed for such a form of settlement ? The prospect of a fair return would be far too remote ; the investment, viewed commercially, would be almost worthless. In a limited way and for people possessed of some means of their own and, what is more, some knowledge of what they are to do, assisted settlement on prepared farms is entirely feasible. It is not only feasible, but it is being done with practical success. But the whole possible scale of it is too small to count. As a solution for the Empire settlement problem it is nowhere.

In other words, it is necessary in our theories of emigration to get away from the " agricultural fallacy ". The experience of the United States in the settlement of the fertile " middle west ", the

Mississippi Valley, led to false conclusions and gave a false bias to migration ever since. In the days of American expansion in the latter part of the nineteenth century it was possible for agricultural immigrants to come into new country in a single flock, raising the single product grain and subsisting off an unlimited world market. That day is all past. There are now in North America—certainly in the United States—too many farmers. The very progress made in the technique of their industry, the wonderful farm machinery, the " rationalization " of agricultural production cuts into their existence. A farmer using a " tractor " can plough at least six acres to one against a farmer with a team. An American farmer working with machinery raises a bushel of wheat off half a square chain of land —the twentieth part of an acre. He can plough this in two minutes, harrow it in two minutes, then go away for four months on a vacation, and when he comes back cut the grain in two minutes, haul and thrash it in four final minutes, thus producing a bushel of wheat with ten minutes' work. To grow wheat it only needs an average of one man for about 250 acres. The output of the average American farmer rose forty-seven per cent from 1900 to 1925. As a result, from 1919 to 1927 4,000,000 people in the United States gave up farming and 19,000,000 acres went out of cultivation. All of such things and many more in regard to the technical aspect of farming can be read in the report of the National Industrial Conference Board of the United States. At every stage and in every operation of farming the marvellous American genius for invention substitutes the machine for the man. There are nearly a million tractors on the American farms. One and the same machine with a few magic adjustments turns itself into a plough or harrows, or a planting-machine or a mower. The machine called a " combine " can cut and thrash the grain all as one job and can tackle soy beans and sweet clover. The economic world is a strange paradox. The more we improve our powers of production, the fiercer seems to grow the fight for life. We cannot use the means we have. Abundance brings poverty. A blessed harvest spells ruin. And labour saving leaves the labourers to starve. The truth is that we are as ignorant of economics as people before Isaac Newton were ignorant of physics. This is not an exaggeration. It is a fact. Economics is not the name of a science but of a problem. And no one has solved it. The position of the American farmer results in a fierce fight against every intrusion upon his market. He must keep it all to himself. No foreigner must sell food or grain or meat or eggs to anyone in the four corners of the Republic. The " agricultural protection " of the platforms of thirty years ago has turned into agricultural exclusion. The tariff bills of the present year (1930) are meant to shut out anything and everything. If one fails to do it, the next one will succeed. For us in the Empire all this stands as a warning. The sooner the Canadian people cut loose entirely from the American agricultural market the better. They can never have it, or only at the price of reciprocity, amalgamation and the girdle of the eighteenth amendment wound round the Continent.

Our policy must rest on different and larger ideas. Our migration *must open its own market*—the secret of it lies in that. It must be so varied AND multiform that every part of it is the market for every other. To try to make a whole nation of farmers, in the days that are, is as hopeless as to make a whole nation of hairdressers. The attempt to expand grain-farming in the west of Canada without expanding other things with it and co-ordinating it with the outside—this means bankruptcy. The shadow of it falls in front of us now as we walk forward.

. . . .

So, then, our companies set to work and bring with them into the area of their operations the landless, jobless man : and his family, if he has one. An immigration policy, to be sound, must be based on the family, not on the detached worker. The man thus brought works for wages. At the start he owns nothing—neither house, nor land nor capital. How can he ? He begins from nothing. The immigrant must not only work for wages, but he must work for what seems low wages. His initial wages must take into account the fact that the company has transported him free of cost and has supplied him with shelter, perhaps with clothes—in fact, has given him a start. He begins in debt. This is deducted from his wages, so that he works for an initial period for what is lower in money than a current union wage, but more than equal to it if we add, in the transport for himself and his family, the temporary maintenance and the guarantee of work. On this basis the company can make money out of his work and pay dividends to the investor.

Such a proposal, to those who know history, looks at first sight like the " indentured labour " of the Virginia colonial days, of the transported criminals of Botany Bay and the Chinese labour of the Transvaal. But there is no real analogy. One case represents coercion and exploitation ; the other assistance. The man under a contract is only working, as most of us work, with a definite job to do and no immediate legal right to quit it. If the company immigrant " quits " his job, let him go. There need be no recourse against him in the criminal law except to forbid him in the future from making a valid contract for wages or for collecting debts. Also let him for the future starve if he wants to ; he has lost his social right of participation.

But there is no need to confuse a scheme of migration with a wilderness of regulations and pains and penalties. Social organization should start with the honest man. Let the other sink.

Nor need the position of any immigrant labourer's lot long remain an inferior one. As soon as his initial debit is cleared his wages will be ample ; there is no reason why he should not receive a free grant of land, if he wants it, when he has saved the means to work it. Nor is there any reason why the company should not give him, even from the start, a payment in its common stock, small but accumulating, that will turn him from a hireling into a partner. This is done already in a number of Canadian and American companies. Such a feature could easily be taken over and incorporated in the plan of a concession company.

.   .   .   .

Some of the companies thus incorporated to bring out emigrants, absorb the unemployed of the Dominions in return for privileges and monopolies, may fail. Indeed, it is inevitable that some would fail. Even with best of legislation and supervision the objects pursued, though honest, may be entirely chimerical. Some of the companies may be so foolishly advised and so insanely conducted as to lose every cent that is put into them. But even here the loss is not complete. John Stuart Mill would have said so. But many economists of to-day would doubt it. At least the operations of the company would shift the money from the investors to the employees. The money would have been "spent" without a productive return. Mill thought this waste and said so. Mill thought, and all the economists of his time at least tried to think, that a mere demand for labour—money spent on labour—was useless unless the labour made something useful. According to Mill, the spendthrift who called for champagne and cigars and then consumed them was of no benefit to society. He merely turned labour into smoke and bubbles. According to Mill, the heavy snowstorm that "makes work" for 10,000 men in a Canadian city was a dead loss to society, not a benefit. According to Mill, the hailstorm that breaks all the glass in a rich man's conservatory, and thus sets a band of glaziers busily to work, is a mere example of destruction which has to be made good. The glaziers never accepted this theory. Indeed, popular prejudice, as opposed to text-book economics, always favoured anything that "made work" and stimulated trade.

Popular prejudice was right. Mill's theory would be correct in a world in which there was no unemployment and in which demand and supply, production and consumption were held in a beautifully balanced equipoise. In a real world there is another element to be considered, what one might call " economic impetus ". By this we mean the value of " starting something ". A pebble rolling down a slope may hit and start a big stone, that rolls and launches a rock and sets in movement an avalanche. Punching through a dike a hole an inch in diameter may start a torrent of water moving that will flood a valley. One feeble joke at a dull dinner may unloose a flood of merriment. So, too, in the economic world. All industry hangs together. Where one stumbles, it affects the next, and presently all fall. Where one quickens the others start to life. The consumer of one is the producer of the other. The spendthrift smoking his cigar sets to work the unemployed cigar-maker, who starts into activity the unemployed baker, who rouses the miller, who wakes up the farmer, who starts the agricultural-instrument maker, who pays the dividends that go to the spendthrift, who buys the cigars that start the cigar-maker and so on. The House-that-Jack-Built, in point of continuous concatenation of consequences, is nothing to the economic world of to-day. When the economic theory of impetus is fully analysed and fully written out it may be found to contain in it the missing elements needed for the solution of the economic paradox.

. . . .

Here then is a general plan for imperial concession

companies, great or small, working with investor's capital, gathered anywhere and everywhere, supplying work, moving workers, exploiting resources— in a word, " starting something ".

They can begin on a big scale or a little, by the action of one government, or two together, or all together.

Many people instinctively hate the idea of companies with concessions of privilege and monopoly. It seems like trading away the " people's rights " to the gifts of nature. It is. And when the people in question are mostly two or three thousand miles away from their rights, haven't used their rights for a hundred years, have no work and no chance of any, the best thing that one can do with their rights is to trade them. At any rate, all the concessions given can be terminable. They can revert to the State at a valuation after fifty years or a hundred years—some day.

So much for the work to be done and the general method of doing it. Let us turn to the investor and consider his run for his money. In a sporting race like the British, that is all he asks, a " run for his money ". Will he get it ?

CHAPTER III

THE INTEGRATION OF CREDIT, CURRENCY, AND CAPITAL

IN the matter of credit, currency and capital, as in all else, the situation of the British Empire presents a bewildering disintegration. As in all else, if the difficulties can be surmounted, the integration of these elements would give stimulus, strength and stability. The British Empire, as such, has no public debt and makes no use of its public credit. In the Empire there is not one public debt, but thirty-seven. There is the debt of Great Britain and Northern Ireland, amounting to about £7,631,000,000 ; the public debt of India £743,250,000 ; a public debt for each of the Dominions—Canada, Newfoundland, Australia, New Zealand, South Africa and the Irish Free State : for the near-dominion, Southern Rhodesia ; for the representative colonies, the Bahamas, Barbados, Bermudas, etc. ; and for a long list of minor colonies and dependencies such as is furnished in the *Statesman's Year Book* or any similar compilation. The grand total runs to £9,955,205,000.

PUBLIC DEBT OF THE BRITISH EMPIRE AS COMPILED IN THE *STATESMAN'S YEAR BOOK* OF 1929

	£
Great Britain and Northern Ireland. .	7,631,000,000
EUROPE :	
Irish Free State	17,000,000
ASIA :	
Borneo, Brunei, and Sarawak . .	49,000
Ceylon.	12,657,000
Cyprus	180,000
Hong-Kong	342,000
India	743,250,000
Straits Settlements . . .	25,654,000
Federated Malay States . . .	9,355,000
Other Malay States . . .	729,000
AFRICA :	
Kenya Colony and Protectorate . .	10,000,000
Uganda Protectorate . . .	1,108,000
Zanzibar	100,000
Mauritius and Dependencies . . .	1,766,000
Nyasaland Protectorate . . .	775,000
Seychelles	4,000
Southern Rhodesia . . .	4,095,000
Swaziland	55,000
Union of South Africa . . .	223,233,000
Nigeria	23,559,000
Gamba	84,000
Gold Coast and Protectorate . .	11,791,000
Sierra Leone and Protectorate . .	1,730,000
AMERICA :	
Bermudas	70,000
Canada	463,198,000
British Guiana	2,675,000
British Honduras . . .	327,000
Newfoundland and Labrador . .	15,004,000
Bahamas	176,000
Barbados	591,000

America—*continued*

Jamaica, etc.	.	.	.	.	4,922,000
Leeward Islands	.	.	.	.	289,000
Trinidad	.	.	.	.	3,282,000
Windward Islands	.	.	.	.	476,000

AUSTRALIA :

Australian Commonwealth	.	.	.	494,129,000
New Zealand	.	.	.	.	251,396,000
Fiji	.	.	.	.	.	154,000

£9,955,205,000

For the present purpose it does not matter whether the compilation in the table is absolutely and exactly up to date. It is the principle of the thing which is under discussion. What I want to show is that there is here an absolutely unused asset, of vast money value—namely, the collective credit of the British Empire. The present debts of Great Britain and the Dominions are separate debts. We in Canada are not liable for the payment of the debt of the United Kingdom, and the United Kingdom is not responsible for the payment of our Canadian debt nor of the Australian. Credit in the Empire has been carefully cut up into bits like everything else. At the present time the public debt of the United States stands (1929) at about $16,500,000,000. The credit of the United States to-day is higher than that of any other country. This does not necessarily arise from the fact that the United States is richer—when wealth is computed in available monetary value—than any other country. It means that in the judgment of those who have funds to lend the United States is more likely to repay its debts and fulfil its obligations than any other country.

The relative credit of the United States and the United Kingdom and other countries can easily be compared. It is only necessary to know what rate per cent is payable as interest on their securities and how much investors are willing to pay to get them. In the spring of 1930 United States taxable securities are sold at a rate that will bring to the purchaser an income of four per cent, or less, on his investment. Other Governments can only get money at higher rates than this. The arithmetic of the matter is complicated by the varying termination dates of the loans ; but the general comparison of present values would show that the United Kingdom and Canada have to pay five per cent at their present credit, Australia nearly five and a half, and all other British Dominions at rates above five per cent.

The details of the case and the temporary fluctuations from day to day are of no import to the present discussion. The broad general conclusion emerges that the United States can borrow money at a rate about one per cent lower than can the United Kingdom or any constituent of the British Empire. But if all the public debts of the United Kingdom and of the Dominions were pooled into a single Empire debt, with all the financial power and tax resources and national wealth and assets of the Empire behind it, the situation would look very different. Without a doubt the credit of such an amalgamation would stand higher than the credit of each and any of its components. Two and two, as often happens, would make more than four.

In practice it would not be possible to pool the entire debt. There would be too much squabbling over the process. But it would be possible—it would be very easy—to create a guaranteed Empire debt to consist of a part—one could easily say, one-half—of the debts of the United Kingdom and the Dominions. India could be left out. Its place in the Empire is too problematical. Any constituent commonwealth which wanted to might stay out. The Irish Free State probably would do so. As yet the modest efforts of the Free State in five years had only raised a debt by March 1927 of £17,000,000 or about £5 14s. per capita. The Canadians have a Dominion net debt of about $280 per capita which the Irish might not be willing to share. But if they did refuse it would only be by misunderstanding the nature of the operation proposed. This is not really a question of sharing another person's debt, but sharing along with other persons the alleviation of part of a debt, without any cost whatsoever. It is, in other words, a piece of financial magic in which something is got out of nothing.

Let me show by an illustration what would happen. When the Canadian Confederation was formed the British Government felt itself interested in effecting the union of the provinces as a matter of Imperial defence. It therefore undertook, as an inducement towards confederation, to guarantee the interest on a loan raised to build a railway to connect (Central) Canada with the sea—the Intercolonial Railway. On the strength of this guarantee the Dominion of

Canada borrowed £3,000,000 at three per cent, whereas its other and ordinary borrowings of the period were at the rate of over six. The guarantee never cost the British Government anything more than words and ink. To consolidate the Empire debt, or part or half of it, it would not be necessary to alter in any way the present mechanism of paying interest. All that would be needed would be for the United Kingdom to guarantee, say, $1,500,000,000 of the public debt of Canada, and Canada to guarantee a similar proportion of the British debt. It would be a mutual guarantee of each for all and of all for each. The current burden of interest would fall just in the same proportion as now, but in each case it would be lighter. The conversion could not be forced. But each Government could take advantage of the termination of each loan as it fell in to pay it off with money borrowed at a lower rate. A lifting of general Empire credit by even one-half of one per cent would affect a colossal saving on the total—indeed, about $300,000,000 a year.

It would be wiser to issue Empire-guaranteed loans in a distinctive and recognizable form, with a special kind of scrip and a special terminology. Forms count, and the visual symbol of a thing is often needed for its appreciation. But the general plan of what to do is among the simplest, the most immediate and the most certain of the means of Imperial integration.

. . . .

A still further strengthening and consolidation of Empire credit could be brought about by amalgamating into a guaranteed issue all the redeemable

Government paper money of the United Kingdom and the Dominions. At the present time each of these constituent parts of the Empire, apart from bank-notes, issues paper money which, in theory at any rate, is redeemable in gold coin. In the case of Canada the redemption has shown itself recently (1929) to be theoretical rather than actual. The fall of the Canadian currency to a discount of two per cent as compared with United States currency was a serious blow to the credit and the investment market of the Dominion. It is as difficult as it is needless to say just how this depreciation could have happened in a country as soundly based and as solvent as Canada, in which the Treasury could easily buy, borrow, or mint enough gold to answer any fluctuation of the exchanges. In this as in other countries there is, of course, a standing temptation to inflation of this sort. The rising value of the United States dollar when bought with Canadian funds tends to check purchases of American goods and tends to favour the Canadian manufacturer. But any advantage of this sort is transitory and illusive. Any possible gain is offset a hundred times by the harm done to national credit, which checks investment at the source. The worst thing that can happen financially to Canada is that it should compare with the United States as a country of ramshackle finance beside a country of absolute integrity where a promise to pay means payment. Those who look back and remember the discredit cast on all American investment and enterprise by the threatening shadow of depreciated silver currency in the 'nineties, and then contrast the situation with the solidity of American monetary structure of to-day, will need no further lesson in the point.

The maintenance of the gold standard is absolutely vital to financial stability. Economists dream in vain of a system of regulated currency without gold, under which an impossibly sagacious board of men, inconceivably above private interest, control the rise and fall of credit and prices as one turns on a tap or tunes a piano. Such a system, if it ever came into operation, would supply new and glorious opportunities for fraud beside which anything now in Wall Street would look like a Sunday school. The only basis for value is in fact, and a gold coin with a mint behind it is a fact. The return from the delirium of war inflation to the sanity of gold redemption was as necessary as it was bitter.

Nor would there be any better way of enduring the gold standard in the Empire than to consolidate by a general guarantee of redemption the paper-money issues of the Empire Governments. As beside the guarantee of the debt, this would only be a minor operation. The very solidity of the guarantee would prevent a rush anywhere for redemption of notes in gold. New issues would have to be accepted for each constituent of the Empire by all the others on terms agreed. But that would only serve to make the issues all the sounder.

·   ·   ·   ·   ·   ·   ·   ·   ·

There can be no doubt that the unity of Empire finance and trade would be greatly assisted if it were possible to go further than this and to establish a uniform system of money and measures. It is, of course, true that as long as each constituent of the Empire maintains in law and practice an accepted gold standard, the particular units of the coinage make no difference to the mechanism of the exchanges. This is true all the world over. British gold sovereigns, American gold dollars, along with gold francs of the present, gold roubles of the past and ingots of new gold from the mines, all form a universal currency. Hence in a purely theoretical way it might be said not to matter if England and Australia count in sovereigns and Canada and Singapore count in dollars. But in practice it matters a whole lot. The common mass of people are actuated by ideas and appearances as well as by realities. The aspect of a single gold coinage, stamped indifferently at Ottawa or London or Melbourne or Pretoria, everywhere the same, everywhere legal tender and everywhere the basis of public credit, would be most impressive for the stability of the Empire. It would serve every day as an outward and visible symbol of the tremendous latent wealth upon which such a monetary system is based.

Unification of the coinage and currency of the Empire would mean that either dollars and cents or else pounds, shillings and pence have got to be abandoned. There is no question which of these two currencies ought to be thrown overboard. It is true that pounds, shillings and pence are overwhelmingly the currency of the British Empire. The dollar is used only in Canada, Newfoundland, the Straits Settlements, Hong-Kong, and in a secondary way in the West Indies. But there is no comparison between the two currencies in point of commercial convenience and common sense. Counting in pounds, shillings and pence is as out of date and as inadequate as Japanese picture writing and the Turkish current script. The Japanese, we are told, realize the defect of their system and will shortly change it. In Turkey, Mustapha Kemel Pasha has already burnt his books behind him and set a whole generation of little Turks fumbling and mumbling their way into phonetics. It is time that England imitated such a forceful outlook, and such willingness to make a present sacrifice for a final gain.

Pounds, shillings and pence were right enough before the Hindoos and the Arabs brought the decimal system of place numbers into Europe. Till then, people only counted in a clumsy way, with fingers, with little sticks, with tallies, or with an abacus, and multiplication was beyond the common man. The Arabic notation was familiar to European scholars as early as the year 1400, but in England, until well into Tudor times, the accounts of manors and parishes and even of monasteries and colleges were kept in Roman figures. Even when the decimal system of counting was introduced, the money of England remained in its primitive multiples of the dozen and the score. The Spaniards, on the other hand, fitted their money to the new arithmetic and from them the thaler and the centavo—the dollar and the cent—went round the world. Spain gave the system to the new world where it appears in decimal currencies of the United States and all of

Latin America. The French Revolution gave it to France, from which it spread later to the Latin Union of Belgium, Italy and Switzerland (1865), to Germany under the Empire, 1875, to Austria and Hungary in 1870, Japan in 1871 and Russia in 1897. England alone goes on counting on its fingers and scratching its head when it vainly tries to multiply a penny halfpenny by five and a half per cent.

Most people in England seem to be unaware of the clumsiness of their money. Visitors from the United States and Canada watch their money calculations with an admiring despair. How do they do it ? If a person lays down a sovereign at a railway station and asks for two adult tickets and one half-ticket at £1 3s. 2d. per ticket, how is it possible that the booking-clerk can hand back with lightning rapidity whatever he does hand back. Perhaps they just guess it. But there is no doubt that even with the utmost development of skill in counting there are lots of operations very simple to us in America and very useful in business which cannot be done in England. A Canadian departmental store can mark down a whole counter full, or a whole store full of goods, with the simple sign " 20 per cent reduction ". The humblest of its customers can calculate the new price from the old ticket. A Canadian tax authority can put on a two per cent or five per cent sales tax above a current price. Imagine in England trying to calculate a five per cent tax on a pair of pyjamas costing 17s. 7½d. and bought at a January reduction sale at a twenty per cent discount. English money clogs external trade. On my desk as I write is a beautiful illus-

trated flower and seed catalogue for 1930 just
arrived in Canada from a great English firm and
calculated to fascinate the eye of the amateur gar-
dener. Such wonderful Antirrhinum at one and
six ! Acquilegia at sixpence and Calendula—the
hardy annual variety—as low as threepence ! One
wonders whether those who make up this catalogue
with a convenient order list with columns for pounds
and shillings and pence realize what a hindrance
this stubborn money with its impossible arithmetic
is to the 10,000,000 prospective customers in Canada.
English money could, of course, be decimalized
without turning it into Canadian and American
dollars. If a shilling was declared to be tenpence
instead of twelve and if ten shillings (the half-
sovereign) were given a name and called let us say
a Royal, or a George, or something equally loyal
and appropriate, the money would run at once into
decimals. This would very little disturb existing
accounts since sovereigns would only need to be
divided by two. On outstanding debts read from
the old currency to the new. The maximum loss,
however great, would be only twopence on the odd
pennies over the last shilling, and even that could
be avoided.

But the result would be incomplete. The Empire
would still be divided with Canada and Newfoundland set against the other Dominions. Far better
incur the full difficulty and get it over and done
with and get a decimal currency and Empire coinage
and Empire credit all consolidated into a rock of
security.

There is a further reason for doing so. Everything that helps to increase the credit and stability of the Empire also helps to draw capital from abroad for investment in the Empire. The existence of a gold standard, the certainty of the payment of all interest on all Government debts in a currency that can be redeemed in gold, lends a further inducement to the outside capitalist over and above that offered by the natural opportunities of physical development. If the economic policy of the British Empire is properly directed from now on, British capital will find its natural investment in the Dominions and, in addition to this, large sums of capital will come in from foreign countries. The situation of a century ago will be exactly reversed. At that period the British productive surplus of capital went abroad to develop foreign countries. Now, that of foreign countries can be, and ought to be, turned into the British Empire. This is, of course, overwhelmingly the case with the United States from which a great flow of capital is already moving every year into British Dominions—Canada, Newfoundland, and to a smaller extent elsewhere. But the same thing will presently happen with Germany and with France as soon as the economic restoration of Europe is complete. The opportunities for investment are not only great, but will grow greater with every decade. They will offer also an element of security that is lacking in investment in cruder and more disturbed countries. It is the proper business of British policy to foresee and prepare for this, to decide whether we want the capital and on what conditions we will permit its investment.

American investment in Canada has already gone a long way, and is viewed with alternating enthusiasm and apprehension. Abundant statistics in this matter are available through the investigations of Mr. F. W. Field, Professor Viner, Mr. A. Kirschberg and other economic specialists. The whole movement is very recent. It only began in any serious proportions in the last five years of the nineteenth century (1896–1900), when American investment in Canadian mines, lumber companies, etc., together with the American building and holding of the Canada Southern (part of the Michigan Central) and other railway ownership, brought the total of investment up to some $150,000,000. From the beginning of the century until the War it increased continuously and rapidly. American interest in the pulp and paper industry represented a factor of increasing importance. There was no doubt also that it was greatly stimulated by the existence of the Canadian tariff, without which American investment would have had no need to enter into Canadian industry and manufacture. The pre-War tariff of Canada against the United States represented an ad valorem duty of about thirty-six per cent. The wall was too high to scale, except with slaughter prices and subsidized exports, and the Canadian anti-dumping legislation of 1907 prevented this form of invasion of the market. The existence of the British preference operated also to draw United States concerns into Canada as a basis from which to sell to Great Britain. This investment of capital from the United States assumed in larger and larger proportion the form of establishing branch factories and branch distribution houses inside the Dominion. This contrasts strongly with the investment of British capital which consists overwhelmingly in the purchase of Government securities, municipal loans and the stock of railway and public utility companies. It is the form of investment which prefers safety to adventure, and where the aim is not so much to make money as to keep it without losing it. Till the re-distribution of all social values effected by the Great War, England possessed, more than any other country in the world, an investing class, consisting of people of limited means. The money of these people came to them by descent and they knew more of Latin Iambics than of business. With them was a landed gentry whose only flight of business enterprise was the pursuit of agriculture by proxy. These people, in their other aspects, were the pride and bulwark of England. They wrote its poetry, they preached its sermons and they fought and won its battles. But of business they knew nothing. Beside them, the leaders and magnates of the business world used to be a mere minority, viewed with a mixture of contempt, awe and envy. This investing class of financially ignorant people, anxious only to keep their money and not hoping to increase it, set the peculiar tone to British investment which still shows itself in the location of British capital in Canada. The reports of the last volume of the *Canada Year Book* show that as computed up to 1927, the total investment of British capital in Canada was $2,192,467,000, of which $1,546,671,000 was placed in Government railway and utility securities and only $645,796,000 in the more " speculative " investment in pulp, paper, mines industries, trade, financial and insurance companies and land. Of the United States total of $3,069,181,000, the speculative investments absorbed $1,518,113,000.

Circumstances naturally favour American investment, especially in the form of branch factories. The people of Central Canada and their neighbours across the lakes are socially much alike. Young men move easily back and forward with no great sense of displacement. Families migrate easily. Till the advent of the prohibition law there was no great and obvious difference of social environment. The training of young men in engineering and in commerce is almost identical. Labour itself is internationally organized, and the methods of business, the forms of laws, and the mechanism and the processes of manufacture practically the same.

This influx of American capital, if we so will it, is only beginning. The proximate development of the north-west of Canada can absorb for years to come all the capital available both in Great Britain and in the United States. In the case of Great Britain our course is obvious. We want the British people's money and we want it all, and themselves with it. What about the Americans ?

The fear is constantly expressed that American capital means American control ; that the American " penetration " of Canada industrially means American penetration politically ; that ultimately the result might be the absorption of Canada into the Republic. From all of this I disagree entirely. Canada is not Nicaragua. There is in this country a sufficient urge and power to keep outside dominance at arm's length. When Americans' money builds in Canada a huge power plant, or a paper mill, what has really happened ? A physical change, a physical improvement that has taken place in Canada ; a new productive resource, as new equipment has been made on Canadian soil. And in the United States, what change ? Nothing. Only " ownership " for which each year they get a bundle of paper sent to them. If their engineers and workmen come into Canada they, or at least their children, turn into Canadians. There is no fear of such a flood of Americans entering this country as to stampede it away to the United States, carrying with it all the British and Canadian subjects of King George. Nicaragua is a little country in the jungle. An American banker can put it in his pocket and so away with it. The republic of Colombia was crooked and rapacious, and so President Roosevelt took away Panama and the Canal zone. Haiti was quarrelsome and murderous, and so American marines and bankers had to land to keep order. The rightness and wrongness of all these things does not concern us here. They belong under the topic, nobly called the White Man's Burden, and the British people—or at least the ones in Great Britain—bear it just as nobly as the Americans do. But Canada is never destined to be a White Man's Burden to the United States. There is no fear of the Americans who come up to Canada absorbing anything, except as under the liquor control acts of the province. On the contrary, they easily, willingly and cheerfully get absorbed themselves.

CHAPTER IV

THE INTELLECTUAL UNITY OF THE EMPIRE

THERE is another aspect of the British Empire and the British people not yet treated, except incidentally, in this book. All that has gone before has been mainly a material discussion of material things—wealth, land, trade and settlement. These things are the first basis of human happiness and progress. But they are not the whole of it. There remains the realm of the mind—the sphere of art and letters, of education, thought, and culture. Which sphere is the more important it is not necessary to discuss. A full dinner pail may be better than an essay on philosophy or it may not ; but it is at any rate necessary to give some consideration to the aspect of intellectual life in relation to the unity of the Empire. We must consider whether any positive and co-operative action can be taken to increase the unity of thought, the unity of culture, of arts and letters among the British peoples.

.   .   .   .

Here again, as in so much else, the United States and the British Empire offer a great and increasing contrast. In the States education and intellectual life are standardized and uniform to the last degree. In the British Empire, as a whole, there is but little intellectual unity and almost no standardization. Only in Canada, owing to the proximity of the United States, does the idea of uniformity and standardization in education make much progress, and even there it encounters a good deal of opposition. The present question, therefore, is whether the integration and unity of the British Empire necessitates on our part an attempt to render our education uniform, and to standardize the work of our schools and colleges into adjustable parts, so that a graduate from Cape Town can fill a position as a teacher in Saskatoon and an engineer from Sheffield build a bridge in Alberta. Over and above the mere technique and programme of education, to what extent should we try to harmonize and standardize our culture ?

In the United States standardization has gone to terrific lengths with an extraordinary effect on the unity and consolidation of the country. The process indicated was taken over into education from large-scale industry where standardization has proved a leading factor in mass production. As has already been said in an earlier part of this book, the system of standardization achieves a marvellous accuracy in machine production. All parts and sections of things manufactured are cut so exactly alike that any one fits in anywhere as an adjustable part. The machines which grind axles and similar steel parts make them true to the one-ten-thousandth of an inch. An American micrometer will measure an error ten times as small as that, the one-hundredth-thousandth part of an inch ! All this means that " parts " can be manufactured on a vast scale, each one without any reference to the machine into which it will be adjusted. Each one is the same as every other one—one would almost say like " peas in a pod "—except that nature's clumsy handiwork cannot compare with American machine production. Everyone knows how standardization has reached its acme in the production of the motor-car. All the world has read of the Ford car, beginning as a poor inchoate skeleton moving along a little track, to receive in turn its body, its engine, its hood, its bolts, its nuts, its glass, its paint, its varnish, at the hands of standardized workmen, who roll along with it, till at the end it passes into life, a finished car, as utterly without individuality of its own as some of the men who make it. There can be no doubt as to the physical and commercial effectiveness of standardization as applied to industry and commerce. It is doubtful, more than doubtful, whether its results are so happy when applied to culture, art and education. It is a wonderful thing so to train the consumer that he wants only the standardized inter-changeable article. This cuts down the need for varieties, makes every stock of articles good every-where and simplifies and cheapens production. It is, no doubt, an excellent thing that now, as said in an earlier chapter, there are in the United States only five kinds of paving-bricks instead of the sixty that there used to be ; that instead of the seven hundred patterns of hotel china that existed a few years ago there are now only one hundred and sixty ; that the sixty-seven kinds of hospital beds have been reduced to four, and the varieties of milk-bottle tops cut down to one. But is it quite so happy that the varieties of Sunday newspapers in the United States have been cut to a single type ; that the editorials, the feature articles, the comic strips and the sob-stuff are all faithfully reproduced in adjustable parts from Maine to California ? The Sunday Press of the United States that consumes a forest every week to make its paper, that is carried in car-load lots through the United States and to which is devoted all the brains and all the technical art that can be bought for money, is a merely huge mass of standardized material, possessing a bewildering bulk but always and everywhere the same. The trouble is that it cannot exist on mass production unless it can train consumers in millions to look at the same thing, laugh at the same thing, cry at the same thing. It is compelled to give the public what it wants. Real literary progress and eminence is found in giving the public what it does not want.

So, too, with American education. From their earliest colonial days the American people have realized the value of the school and college. They made great sacrifices even in the hardest days of their first settlement, to get schools and teachers for their children. The " school teacher " and the " school marm " of New England are among the honoured characters of American history. The result is seen in a people who from the very first were literate, whose book knowledge could join with their native ingenuity in making machines, whose " spelling book " and whose ability to " cypher " enabled them to subdue nature with the power of mechanical knowledge. Two centuries and a half passed by, and then the Spirit of Machinery in its turn came to give its reward to the people who had made it. It offered to apply to the whole of their education the wonderful process of mass production, adjustable parts and standardized products which had made the industrial fortune of the nation. The American people are accepting the gift, rapidly and eagerly, spreading abroad standardized education and culture from East to West, from North to South, till the schools and the colleges like the Sunday papers are all turning into one vast uniformity. All this is only a theory of the immediate present, with its results still in the future.

. . . .

In the history of modern education there was for long centuries no uniformity standard nor rule at all. Oxford from its beginnings under Henry III for 300 years never held any written examinations. Shakespeare and Milton, Isaac Newton and Adam Smith were all educated in different ways. Westminster school was not at all like Eton School, and no one wanted it to be. There were no technical qualifications for entry into anything except for the law and for medicines ; for the law by eating so many dinners, for medicine by walking a hospital. Entry to the army was by being born of the right parents. There were no standardized matriculations, credits, units, courses, half-courses, semisters, equivalents, protantos and prerequisites. As for the poor, education was not for them, except to lead them out of danger into a monastery.

In point of uniformity, education in England was a mere welter till at least the middle of the nineteenth century, with no " public schools ", in the

North American sense, till the year 1870. In America, education was far more uniform from the first because it had to rely upon legislation. But it was, until the present generation, far more diversified and varied than it is now. Indeed until very recently education everywhere, and in England more than in America, was in need of system, of organization, of standards. The danger is that we may now run to the other extreme.

The standardization of education is a thing of our immediate time, a present problem with no past parallel, a small cloud of danger which may later on obscure the sky. On this continent, at least, we are so anxious to make the entry into all professions a matter of provable merit that we are trying to cut and dry every performance, to indicate exactly the content of each branch and part of knowledge, to leave nothing to the individual spontaneity of the teacher and the pupil, with the result that a huge educational machine is being created from Maine to California and from Halifax to Vancouver in which every teacher is going to be like every other teacher and every text-book the same as every other text-book.

As I see it, this very similarity and uniformity defeats its own end. There is not enough room left for individual variety, individual genius. People of exception to mark the path of the nation are at least as necessary as the mass who trample it smooth. In education spontaneous effort is best brought out by the cultivating of differences not of similarities. One good text-book is not as good as two bad ones. One queer teacher—something of a crank and eccentric—may be of more cultural value than a whole boxful as alike as ninepins. As life becomes more uniform in America, personality, individuality, tends to disappear. America gains, of course, enormously in immediate power from the similarity of its people. There are no revolutions in Boston, no monarchist plots in Idaho. The foreign culture of New Orleans has passed away along with the polygamy of Utah. The South has been northernized and the West has been easternized. Everywhere there are the same schools, colleges, churches, the rotary clubs, and the Y.M.C.A., all constituting the most wonderful political and social unity ever witnessed. In the British Empire there is nothing to compare with it. There is less uniformity in the people as between two neighbouring counties in England than as between Maine and California.

But such cultural results can only be attained at a certain price and risk. Even in industry there is always the lurking fear that standardization may mean stagnation. An industry equipped at vast expense with plant and machinery for one special piece of production in which it creates an unrivalled order and cheapness, cannot well change. China, no doubt, became standardized, in its own humble way, thousands of years ago, and inventive genius languished and died. America not yet. We are told that Mr. Henry Ford relinquished a hundred million dollars in order to change the popular model of the Ford car—a titanic effort against the creeping paralysis of standardization. But the inherent tendency of mass-production to run into a fixed mould and solidity is ever there. It is the ghost behind the scene at the industrial banquet.

. . . .

In the British Empire we are, industrially and culturally, only at the beginning of standardization. In industry, especially in England itself, we need it. There is no doubt, even to outsiders without business experience and technical knowledge, that the industrial plant of England needs to be overhauled and reorganized from top to bottom. It is probable, also, that at present there is not enough uniformity, or rather not enough unity and contact among the varied educational systems of the Empire. There are in existence bodies such as the British Association in which all the Empire shares. There is a conspicuous element of exception in the existence of the Rhodes scholars, past and present, who form, link by link, a sort of intellectual chain of Imperial contact. Medicine and science are more or less assimilated throughout the Empire, but mainly for the reason that they are everywhere international. But in the cultivation of the liberal arts, the education of the arts colleges shows very little contact, very little knowledge of one part of the Empire with another, very little of the mutual support which it ought to be possible to extend. It would not be possible in this book without departing from its proper sphere to attempt to enter the field indicated and to discuss the co-ordination of education throughout the Empire. But there are certain aspects of culture, of literature and art which lie in close connection with economic life, and in which intellectual life and material welfare act and react upon one another. I am thinking here of the field presented by books, songs, dramas, broadcasts and moving pictures. To what extent shall we try to control these things in the interests of Imperial unity ? I am aware that the whole British tradition is in favour of entire freedom in the world of arts and literature, and I am well aware that the republic of letters is a nobler ideal than the stimulation by a forced draught of the ardour of national authorship.

The whole British tradition is in favour of letting people read what they want to read, see what they want to see and hear what they want to hear. If they want to read Norwegian drama and laugh at American humour, let there be no " tax on enlightenment " to stop them from doing so. This is a noble doctrine, a fundamental idea of the British people and, for generations, a bed-rock basis of British public policy. There was no attempt to prohibit or penalize in England the works of Robert Burns or Walter Scott, or to keep Shakespeare out of Scotland. The attitude contrasts with that of many well-meaning people—in Canada, let us say —who look on Canadian authorship as a thing to be encouraged like Canadian cheese and Canadian apples. To them a Peterborough poet is welcomed in the same way as a Peterborough ham, and the consumption of American fiction deplored like the consumption of American pickles.

With such an attitude as this I have no sympathy, except as with the misguided idea of patriotism which lies behind it. But in regard to a large part of the field of literary and cultural output newer

circumstances have arisen to overwhelm and alter
the earlier doctrine of absolute freedom of exchange
and absolute freedom of intercourse. The production of magazines and books, dramas and moving
pictures has now become a series of large-scale
industries, which are no longer mere matters of art
but also large matters of business. In one at least
of these things—the moving picture—the commercial
and economic aspect utterly and absolutely over-
whelms its artistic aspect. A poet writes a poem all
by himself. He doesn't even need a pen and ink.
If too poor to buy a pen and ink he can sing or
recite his poem to any sympathetic ear. No more
than that is needed for art. Even if he writes it
or prints it, that is but a simple matter for a few
copies, and if the virtue is there it will circulate for
its own sake, in wider and wider circles, and if the
virtue is not there the voice of the singer falls
unheard and the paper is lost in the rubbish heap.

But the moving picture. No single Shakespeare
can create one. There must be a vast apparatus
and contraption of cameras, of cardboard towns,
of supers and scenery, and reaching out from the
chains of theatres and tons of advertizing—millions
upon millions of dollars of invested capital. Against
all this, the individual is lost and hopeless. The
doctrine of the freedom of the republic of letters
when applied to the free importation and exhibition
of foreign moving pictures absolutely breaks down.

. . . .

The Americans appreciated and seized and
exploited the moving picture earlier and better
than any other people. They deserve all the credit

that accrues from that. A practical result of this is that now all the world looks at American moving pictures. In England and in the Empire we look at very few others. If we found that all over the Empire we read exclusively American poetry and thought our own to be poor stuff beside it, there would be nothing to do about it except to pray for new brains or emigrate to the United States. But is this so, in regard to moving pictures ? Is there nothing that we can do, or ought to do about it ?

.   .   .   .

The motion picture came into the commercial world under the name of the vitascope in 1896. It showed 1,000 feet of pictures so measured to correspond in time with the " turn " of a vaudeville artist. It showed pictures of moving things—a marvellous novelty ; pictures of a moving train, pictures of horses jumping. It made a vast sensation. Then the novelty wore out, and the flickering black and white pictures lost their attraction. People couldn't sit for ever and watch a photographic train running or see a photographic cow milked in a black and white barnyard. Reality was better. At that stage imagination came to the aid of mechanical invention. A picture was made up (1903) called *The Life of an American Fireman.* Here were seen firemen sliding down a pole, leaping into a wagon, roaring at full speed (13 miles an hour) through the street. A house is seen burning. A woman and child appear at the window. A printed " legend " tells the audience that these are the chief fireman's wife and child. A man going up a ladder, the chief fireman ! A man carrying down a woman and child! Chief fireman eating supper with his rescued family. And with this the "photoplay" came into the world, with an incalculable effect on the character, happiness and destiny of mankind.

.   .   .   .

There is no need to recount the story of the success of the moving picture. All the world knows how it grew from the crude beginnings as the *American Fireman* and the *Great Train Robbery* to the vast Hollywood panoramas of to-day. The point before us at present is that the Americans grasped its full commercial significance and made it their own. The motive was overwhelmingly that of business —how to make money—not art, not patriotism. The motion picture for all its millionaire paraphernalia is the lowest of the arts. It is saturated, permeated, penetrated by the business motive. It is there for money. That is why the industry deserves to be treated not as an art but as a commercial enterprise. I do not mean that the motive force is altogether commercial. The urge of art comes in. Making up a scenario is creative. "Producing" it is creative. The longing of the country girl to be a great screen artist has in it something of the quality of the child who wants to be a painter —that and sheer vanity. But in the motion picture business the true art side is overwhelmed, as I say, by the other factors. The picture is there first, last and foremost to make money. It must avoid anything and everything that doesn't pay. "Art for art's sake" has no meaning when a "production" costs a million dollars.

.   .   .   .

234

The Americans, I repeat, have the credit of having first truly appreciated the possibilities of the moving picture. It had to make its way against the prejudice of the educational classes. It had to appeal to the crowd, to the common people, to the young. Its price was ten cents. At that it needed an audience of many millions. It must suit itself to their taste and level itself to their understanding. Hence at the beginning people who had had a classical and literary education failed to sympathize with the moving picture. Its poor black and white simplicity, its crude pathos, its elementary heroics appealed to the newsboy rather than to the professor. In the long run the newsboy was right and the professor was wrong. People of " classical education " in every age are apt to be impervious to newer forms of art and letters. The mould of their minds is set. In England, at least until yesterday, what is called educated taste in art and letters ruled more than in America where the word " highbrow " sweeps it jeeringly aside. In England the best known magazines, newspapers and reviews are written for educated people only. In America, overwhelmingly and with but few conspicuous exceptions, newspapers and magazines are written for the man on the street. Hence the moving picture found its proper psychological environment for its growth in America and made the United States its home. With each stage of growth it grew further on what it fed on, and fed more and more as it grew. Hence its position became more and more entrenched. Advantages of climate and such were only incidental. Nature has made fifty Hollywoods where commerce selected only one. The real advantage was in the psychological setting—the American mind free from the artistic prejudice of old-world culture; the American mechanical ingenuity to create "fade outs" and "cut backs" and make a ten-story building with one story of it real and the rest in tiny cardboard; and, above all, in the vast American industrial class with its high wages and easy standard of living, and ten cents to spend in tens of millions.

. . . .

So the moving picture is there. Statistics made up a year or so ago, give some idea of its colossal size and the strength of its entrenched position. An average feature picture costs from $200,000 to $300,000. Larger scale productions run up to $2,000,000. Four years ago the investment in the business was estimated at $1,500,000,000 and it increases yearly. One great company alone produces 900,000,000 feet of film a year. About 800,000,000 feet of film is exported every year. There are 50,000 moving picture houses in the world, in the United States 20,000, in Germany 4,000, in France 3,000, in Great Britain 3,500. The great bulk of the supply to these picture theatres is American. The American pictures, carrying with them the American message, American ideas, American goods, American advertising, go all over the world. The Far East took 4,000,000 feet of Americanism in 1913 and absorbed 54,000,000 feet in 1925. In the artistic sense there is no real competitor except Germany; and in the whole matter, as art, as production, as commerce, as influence, England and the English are nowhere.

The only thing more surprising than this is the feeble complacency of the English in accepting it. Such legislation as there is, like the duty on American films, is without real effect ; the fraction per cent law merely induces the American owners of English picture houses to put on a fraction per cent of inferior English stuff beside which the American shines with a bright light.

.   .   .   .

The effect commercially is incalculable. Not only is the industry in itself a huge national asset, but it serves as a huge advertising medium for national goods. To use the true American phrase, it helps to " sell " the United States. Britishers, Australians, Canadians, Polynesians and Turks sit at the picture and admire the smoothly gliding American car, the magnificence of American metropolitan hotels and the luxury of American transport. Beside all this " home " seems but a poor place. There rises and grows the legend of America—great, powerful and luxurious in a broken and beaten world.

.   .   .   .

In this way, the American moving picture flickering away in the dark silence of 50,000 " palaces " converts the world to its ideas, shows to the world the epic pageant of American history, the history of a land of heroes casting out the tyranny of Europe ; shows to the world the Great War won by America ; shows how a great people and a great President, vexed to the heart at the conflicts of a benighted Europe, sent out an army and conquered it, and then, returning home, refused all territory

and all reward, performing its task at cost and
nothing more.

.   .   .   .

In all these there is not meant to be any word of
criticism against the United States. If they set
their history in a high and patriotic light for their
young people they are only doing what every nation
has done, and England as much as any. National
history without a certain infusion of lies would not
be a strong enough stimulant for the young ; or
if not lies, at least a warm and generous colouring
of the truth. I remember that when, as a little
boy in England, I first read of the wars between
England and France, I was given to understand that
the English were always victorious. As soon as
they saw the French they gave one wild " hurrah "
and swept the French off the field. At sea any
French fleet was at once sent to the bottom with
one true British broadside. The history books did
not explain how it was that such poor nuts as the
French were the dominant power in the world for
at least a century. In these books, of course, the
Prussians had no part in winning Waterloo except
a complimentary entrance to shake hands with
Wellington after it was over ; just as in the
American books Cornwallis was conquered by George
Washington without the French fleet that held him
prisoner.

With all of this kind of thing there is no
need to quarrel here. The discussion belongs in
the higher atmosphere of world-wide humanism.
The Americans, in regard to history, to patriotism,
to moving pictures and to the dissemination of

their own ideas and their own standards are only doing what we all do, or would like to.

. . . .

The problem here is to discuss what we are going to do about it. The answer to this question, as I understand it, is the entirely Christian precept to do to the Americans what the Americans would do to us. In the past when the United States found that they could not compete with British cotton and woollen goods because of England's initial advantages and long lead, they shut them out. In the past when the United States found that its makers could not compete with English rails and structural steel and tin plate, they cut them out. In the present when the United States find that their farming class do not want to import Canadian eggs and Canadian cream and Canadian maple sugar, they cut them out.

If any foreign nation had established a moving-picture industry that sent films to the United States, that seized and held the whole market, there is no doubt what they would do or how right they would be in doing it. They would shut it out with whatever duties prohibitions or legislation were necessary to keep it out. Then they would try to build up in their own country a better industry than the one they excluded. That is what they have always done in the past and that is where they have succeeded.

. . . .

Let us suppose then that we exclude from the Empire the American moving picture—not half, not partly, but altogether. Let us suppose that we gave, by joint Empire legislation of the United Kingdom and any participating Dominions, two years' notice, or three if two is not enough. Without such notice the prohibition would merely create disaster for picture-house owners, employees and scores of others. But with two years' notice, or three, the industry can reform and recreate itself on British ground. Leaving out British India there are 66,500,000 white people in the Empire with the " picture habit " already acquired with some 60,000,000 more black and yellow people ready to acquire it. The game is worth the candle, even if the candle is the biggest battery of electric arcs that ever hung in Hollywood. Think what an influx of capital and energy would be let loose by such a project ! The Empire has not one, but a dozen suitable places, there are cloudless climates and desert sand and forests all grouped together as required ; or Arctic snows ready to use if we care to break away from the Hollywood tradition that life all happens in the sunshine. Observe further that under such a plan, with two years' notice, the actors and the personnel have nothing to lose and much to gain. There would be a regular gold rush into the new British movies. We should get back our lost Charlie Chaplins and our Mary Pickfords. British theatre managers would lose nothing : if the pictures were good enough the same public will be there. The gain to British capital and investment would be enormous. But greatest of all would be the gain to British ideals and ideas now dethroned. And if we failed, we could at any moment resume our present humble and admiring status.

CHAPTER V

WHAT TO DO AND HOW TO DO IT: THE WORK OF AN ECONOMIC CONFERENCE

INDIVIDUALS can argue and discuss. Only Governments can act. The steps that may be taken towards the economic integration of the British Empire must be made by the Governments of its constituent units, the United Kingdom and the Dominions. It is generally understood that an Imperial Conference will be called in the near future, and very probably in the current year. This conference, however, from all indications will be chiefly occupied with purely political discussion. It is rumoured that it may undertake to draw up a constitution for the Empire. Inasmuch as the Empire has done without a constitution since its beginning in Saxon times, over a thousand years ago, this would not seem a pressing matter. But a certain section of public opinion in Great Britain and the Dominions is anxious to obtain a more precise definition of the constitutional relation of the United Kingdom and the Dominions than any which exists at present. This is, in reality, asking a more precise definition of the words of the Delphic Oracle, or a legal decision of the riddle of the Sphinx. These relations cannot be stated in exact terms because there are no exact terms in existence to state them in. Each of the Dominions is under the Crown. Each one controls its own local affairs. Each one controls its diplomatic and foreign affairs. Each one controls its commerce. Each one uses a British law-court as a court of final appeal. But this last only because it wishes to. Each one, also, uses the Rules of the St. Andrews Golf Club, and various Dominions make use of the Marquess of Queensberry's rules, and the Base Ball rules of the World Series Organization of the United States.

The question whether this means that the Dominions are independent states can only be answered by saying that the Dominions are Dominions and that the Empire is the Empire. Beyond this all is quibble, confusion and logemachy, and the whole discussion futile. As beside the real question of unemployment, poverty, and the apprehension of commercial decline and economic failure, this sustained discussion of academic theory is worse than futile and becomes detrimental to progress. The politics of the Empire and, above all, of England ought to turn at the present time on economic questions. The urgency is too great to permit of the intrusion of minor things or of things that lie within different spheres. It will be a great disaster for England if a national election is allowed to turn, as certain forecasts have it, on the status and ritual of the Church. These still and sacred mysteries are not for the noise of the hustings.

. . . .

For the economic problem what is needed is to call an Economic Conference of delegates from the

United Kingdom, the Free State, Canada, Newfoundland, South Africa, Australia and New Zealand. There is no place in this for India. None of the Dominions want to link up their economic life with the good will or bad will, the aspirations, the hatreds and the convulsions of the welter of peoples who live in British India and the Indian States. The inclusion of India and the Crown dependencies and half-dependencies in the Economic Conference, of which I speak, would guarantee its failure. What is wanted is a conference between nation and nation, between white men and white men, a Dominions Economic Conference.

.   .   .   .

The work of an economic conference would meet the initial difficulty that there is nobody in existence which can give it any power to act for the Empire as a whole. We have divided the Empire into parts. No one can act for all. The painful beginning to be made amounts in a sense to undoing the work of the past and trying to create by agreement and compact the single action that is lost.

Each Dominion—calling the United Kingdom one, as it ought to be—can appoint a delegation. When the Conference meets it can then receive resolutions to appoint committees to draw up schemes. These can be drafted on the lines of the Naturalization Act and the Empire Settlement Act to become valid when accepted by one or more parliaments of the Dominions. The Conference can approve the schemes and refer them to the parliaments. It would be better to do first the things that are least contentious in aim and least complicated in operation.

FIRST.—Creation of a Consolidated Empire Debt. Resolved, that a committee be appointed to report a plan for the consolidating and refunding of such parts of the debts of the United Kingdom and the Dominions as may be safely guaranteed for all by each, and for each by all.

SECOND.—That a committee report on the extent to which it is feasible to reform the currencies and coinage of the parts of the Empire, with special reference to the introduction of the decimal system, uniform coinage and a unified, guaranteed paper currency.

．　．　．　．　．　．　．　．　．

These two first items are not really difficult to accomplish. They encounter as their principal element of opposition only the force of accumulated inertia. But they do not involve any national danger, and do not turn on any points a really controversial opinion. What follows is much more difficult.

THIRD.—That a committee report a proposal of Empire Tariff Revision, following the general principles of the safeguarding of manufacture in each Dominion, an Empire super-tariff against foreign goods over and above the tariff made by each Dominion, and the right of all the Dominions, including the United Kingdom, to make inside this arrangement any further reciprocal bargain with any foreign country which may serve its commercial interest, so that the Empire tariff is not fixed and obligatory at any time, in any part, on any of the component parts of the Empire.

．　．　．　．　．　．　．　．　．

Round this matter of the tariff would turn the greatest difficulty of Empire Integration, and it would turn not on what Canada or Australia wants, but on the wishes of Great Britain. With the British market wide open to the foreign world any system of Empire preference is of little account. It may be of use or stimulation to certain trades, and is always a noble and fraternal gesture. When an order in council from Canada in 1913 extended an amicable preference to the Friendly Islands, the joy in the South Seas was purely local.

If the argument in this book is sound, the adoption of a reciprocal integrated tariff system in the Empire is the most immediate and most effective means of economic advance. But it is idle to conceal the fact that such a tariff means a break from the Cobdenite doctrine of free trade. It is a sharp alternative, " yes " or a " no ", a division as clear and absolute as the two sides of a knife edge. Only a vote in Great Britain can settle it. Outside of Great Britain, we other British people can only watch and pray.

. . . .

The greatest prospect of Empire Integration lies, however, outside of the tariff system. Even without tariff revision it could be undertaken, though a reciprocal tariff would afford an enormous initial stimulus. This project is the development of the resources of the outside Dominions by the credit, capital, labour of the United Kingdom. This book has attempted to show the means of operation which might be summarised in a conference motion somewhat as follows :

FOURTH.—That a committee be appointed to report a plan of Empire Migration Settlement and Development of Resources, the plan to involve, as its leading features, the investment of private capital from within and without the Empire, the grant of free passages, initial support and work under contract, to British labourers and their families, Government assistance from the Dominions concerned, in the making of surveys, roads, and communication and the creation by Empire Incorporation of privileged companies to undertake the operations of development and settlement on a commercial basis and with a view to a pecuniary return to their shareholders.

．　．　．　．　．　．　．　．　．

These are the proposals towards which the argument and effort of all the preceding chapters have been directed. Few people will agree on the details of each separate plan. But many will join in the earnest desire for human welfare in a United British Commonwealth which is the inspiration of this book.

FINIS

Printed in Great Britain by Butler & Tanner Ltd., Frome and London